The Stamp of Class

The Stamp of Class

Reflections on Poetry & Social Class

Gary Lenhart

THE UNIVERSITY OF
MICHIGAN PRESS
Ann Arbor

Copyright © by the University of Michigan 2006
All rights reserved
Published in the United States of America by
The University of Michigan Press
Manufactured in the United States of America
⊛ Printed on acid-free paper

2009 2008 2007 2006   4 3 2 1

A CIP catalog record for this book is available from the British Library.

Library of Congress Cataloging-in-Publication Data

Lenhart, Gary.
    The stamp of class : reflections on poetry and social class / Gary
Lenhart.
        p.   cm.
    ISBN-13: 978-0-472-09917-7 (acid-free paper)
    ISBN-10: 0-472-09917-5 (acid-free paper)
    ISBN-13: 978-0-472-06917-0 (pbk. : acid-free paper)
    ISBN-10: 0-472-06917-9 (pbk. : acid-free paper)   1. American
poetry—20th century—History and criticism.   2. Working class in
literature.   3. Whitman, Walt, 1819–1892—Political and social
views.   4. Yearsley, Ann, 1753–1806—Criticism and interpretation.
5. Duck, Stephen, 1705–1756—Criticism and interpretation.
6. Literature and society—English-speaking countries.   7. Working
class writings—History and criticism.   8. Social classes in
literature.   I. Title.
PS310.W67.L46 2006   2005016613

To my parents, who provided me with board and plenty of room, tempered my excesses with their love, and continue to serve as models of generosity; and my forbearing daughter and wife, who are my abiding loves and inspiration.

[Edmund] Wilson's article was just half-baked enough to make one warm around the collar. It is so damned easy for such as he, born into easy means, graduated from a fashionable university into a critical chair overlooking Washington Square, etc. to sit tight and hatch little squibs of advice to poets not to be so "professional" as he claims they are, as though all the names he has just mentioned have been as suavely nourished as he—as though 4 out of 5 of them hadn't been damned well forced the major parts of their lives to grub at *any* kind of work they could manage by hook or crook and the fear of hell to secure! Yes, why not step into the State Dept and join the diplomatic corps for a change! indeed, or some other courtly occupation which would bring you into wide and active contact with world affairs! As a matter of fact I'm all too ready to concede that there are several other careers more engaging to follow than that of poetry. But the circumstances of one's birth, the conduct of one's parents, the current economic structure of society and a thousand other factors have as much or more to say about successions to such occupations, the naive volitions of the poet to the contrary.

—Hart Crane

Preface

At the end of eighth grade, the students in my junior high school had to fill out program cards that would determine our high school schedules. We were offered three tracks of study: liberal arts, commercial, or industrial arts. My mother and stepfather knew well what industry was. My mother was widowed at twenty-six when my father jumped from the cab of a ready-mix concrete truck on which the brakes failed. He was killed when the truck veered unpredictably and ended on top of him. Left to raise two small sons (my brother Larry was five, I was six), my mother was fortunate to meet through close neighbors a man who cared for her enough to raise her children as his own. She remarried the following summer.

When my stepfather reacted adversely to the diesel fuel in the Baltimore and Ohio roundhouse and developed skin sores and a painful rash, the railroad's doctors placed a lead mask on his face and irradiated him until whatever was growing on him ceased and desisted, then sent him back to the roundhouse. A few years later, he walked off the Ford assembly line after six months on the job. A quiet man who liked to hunt and fish, he said he just couldn't bear the conditions of factory work. By the time I was in eighth grade, he was employed as a driver for Allied Van Lines, but was only months away from quitting that job too. Despite his complaints, the boss continued to assign a pair of mean-tempered brothers as his helpers. A year after my stepfather quit the job, the brothers were arrested and convicted of rape and murder.

Although my mother wanted something better for her boys, she wasn't eager that we have anything to do with art. She encouraged us at math, but didn't see why I would waste an evening drawing butterflies. She wanted me to become a gentleman, which meant white shirt and tie, a steady income, and sufficient reading skills that no one could bamboozle me with a bum contract. She suggested I sign up for the commercial track.

"But Mrs. Grover said I should take liberal arts." (Mrs. Grover was my homeroom and English teacher.)

"Mrs. Grover is *not* your mother."

But Mrs. Grover was alert, and cared enough about the children in her room to intercept my registration card before it was sent to the office, saying, "You're a bright boy. Don't you want to go to college?"

That night, my mother wished to talk to me alone. She told me that I had at that point gone further in school than anyone in the family, so I shouldn't rely any longer on my parents' guidance: "From now on, you will have to make your own decisions."

At thirteen years old, so far as school went I was a free agent. My parents were devout Roman Catholics; we never missed a holy day of obligation. We didn't have to look for jobs; my mother found them for us and told us when we would start. We didn't have to decide what we would do on weekends; like our parents, if we weren't on the job or playing sports, then we were working around the house. But when it came to school, I could travel as far and wide as I pleased.

That first important encounter with freedom always meant a lot to me, but it's only from a distance that I've appreciated the richness of the event. There's the educational tracking that shunts most working-class kids toward a predictable future, my mother's desire that her sons move up the social ladder, her willingness to sacrifice proximate gratifications to assure that we did, the collision of values that shifts parental authority to agents of the state, the fear of art as exotic and frivolous, the glimpse of education as liberation—and alienation. My mother was the only girl in a family with five boys. Of the seventeen cousins born to those siblings, my brother and I were the only two to attend college. After graduation, we became the only two to move away— far away. Larry went to Los Angeles and I to New York City, he to a career in banking, and I to become a poet. Had she known how far from home our educations would take us, I sometimes wonder whether my mother would have listened to Mrs. Grover.

My parents encouraged us to attend college, but warned that they could provide nothing in way of support except a room at home and ample meals. We had to pay for our own tuition, and there was enough to cover books but not room and board. I accepted a full scholarship to a small Catholic college nearby. Once there, like a rich man I took only the courses that engaged me, without respect to what I would do after graduation or what I might declare as a major. No one ever asked me why I chose to study English instead of another major that promised more income, or teased that I would end up a high school teacher. We respected and admired high school teachers.

When I accepted a scholarship to pursue graduate study in English literature, my parents never questioned my decision or its practicality. I arrived at the University of Wisconsin's Madison campus in 1969. That year there were protests against the Vietnam War, an occupation of the Wisconsin statehouse by supporters of increased benefits for impoverished families, and a sustained campus strike to support the organizers of a teaching assistants union. When I lost the scholarship during the political turmoil of Cambodian Spring because a conservative professor failed me for my participation in the strike, my stepfather only told me that if I was going to carry a picket sign, I should be prepared to use it, and why did I think they put those signs on sticks? After that, I supported my studies by working the night shift at UPS and by washing dishes in a French restaurant. When I left graduate school without a doctorate, my parents weren't disappointed. My mother said they wondered why a twenty-four-year-old man was still in school anyway. Over the next few years, as I devoted myself to poetry, lived in a series of run-down apartments on New York's Lower East Side, and drove cab to pay the rent, my loyal parents defended me to their friends: "He never asks us for a nickel."

After graduating from college I dated a young social worker who generously instructed me in music and art, while smoothing some of my social rough edges. In my life I have been fortunate to meet several women who accepted me as what a basketball coach might call "a project" (i.e., players with "raw" talent who need a lot of work on their game). After twenty years of schooling, I knew how to compose sentences that befitted a graduate student in literature. But I was thirty-two before the woman who became my wife helped me eliminate glaring nonstandard forms of speech that she felt caused people to underestimate my intelligence. It only took about six months of concentrated attention (and my daily exasperation) to eliminate "ain't," for example, from my everyday diction. Soon I was working in publishing and teaching college composition. Though I've taught for the last ten years at Ivy League colleges, the patterns and even the affect of my speech revert to old habits when I spend any time with my family. So much for writing like you talk.

Many years ago Ed Friedman, then director of the Poetry Project at St. Mark's Church in New York City, asked me to organize a panel of poets to talk about poetry and class at the Project's annual symposium. As we mulled over a list of possible participants, we would ask each other, what do you suppose his or her class background is? For the most part we couldn't tell. We weren't looking for uniformity, so it didn't matter. Yet, when I phoned one poet and asked her to be on the panel, she responded warily, "How did you know?" She worried that somehow her speech or demeanor gave her away.

That panel—and that phone call—sparked the meditation that became this book. It's subtitled *Reflections on Poetry and Social Class* to indicate that this is not an exhaustive or definitive study of class effects on poetry, but essays about reading poetry with an awareness of class and class-related themes. When I began research on this project, there were few books to guide me. Tillie Olsen's *Silences* provided a direction, as did Janet Zandy's anthology of working-class women's writing. During the ten years that I have been working on this book, much more has been written about what is now called working-class studies. Pioneering scholarly efforts by Zandy, Constance Coiner, Cary Nelson, Alan Wald, and others have focused for the most part on writers other than those I consider here. I hope that *The Stamp of Class* will contribute to the conversation by reading poets who have yet to be examined in this light. I make no broad claims for this book or the poets it considers, many of whom figure marginally in existing histories. I have written about them simply because their poems inspire me, and can easily imagine another book on this topic addressing an entirely different set of poets.

Larry McMurtry's *Walter Benjamin at the Dairy Queen* recounts his love affair with books and reading, and how that pursuit led him beyond Archer City, Texas, to the world of literature. There are other kinds of writers: the novelist Erskine Caldwell liked to brag, "I don't read books, I write 'em." But all the poets discussed here are enthusiastic, if not erudite, readers. The poet Alice Notley once told me that it was difficult for her husband, Ted Berrigan, to find books he hadn't already read. Walt Whitman tracked the difference between him and his siblings to the library card he received as a young apprentice, which allowed him to read the novels of that "tory and a high church and state man" Walter Scott several times through. Marcia Nardi never had the means to leave the continental United States, but learned French so she could read Corbière. The thresher Stephen Duck carried the *Spectator* into his employer's fields to read during breaks.

McMurtry says in his long essay that although he worked for twenty years as a cowboy, the other cowboys knew he was not really a cowboy, but a reader—that is, someone who found pleasure in that act. The poets discussed herein were born to different social stations; as is common in the United States, some rose and fell in status, often several times, during their lives. All were, however, readers. That contributed to the kinds of poems they wrote and complicated their family, peer, class, and artistic identities.

Reading, and reading poems especially, has always been, and remains, a suspect activity in the U.S.A., and not just among the working class. Several journalists and historians have mentioned the paucity of books in the residences of Presidents Reagan and George H. W. Bush. It may have been in that respect that they were most representative of their constituents. For ten years I worked sporadically as a furniture mover, and I rarely saw many books in people's houses, except in those of Bible salesmen and schoolteachers.

I became a reader after I fractured my skull at six years of age. For several months I was bedridden, and for a year the left side of my face was paralyzed. Because I was unable to attend school or run about, my mother patiently and lovingly taught me to read—mostly comic books, though that Christmas my grandmother gave me a subscription to the *Sporting News*. By that September, when I began first grade for the second time, I had the habit of reading, and have continued in its grip.

This book's title derives not from a poem but from a review by the young journalist Walt Whitman of an exhibition of American painting. Referring to a portrait of a young American boy, Whitman declares the painting unmarred by "the stamp of class" that confines much Old World art. Most of the poets treated in this book, whatever their social origins, shared Whitman's dream of a genuinely democratic and classless society. Many, perhaps all, were eventually disappointed. If there's a thread connecting the various essays in this book, it passes through those dreams and disappointments.

Acknowledgments

Special thanks to Ed Friedman, who started me down this path by inviting me to talk about some of these issues at the Poetry Project Symposium, and to Joel Lewis, who always had something to say about the subject and often guided me to fresh or neglected sources.

Thanks to those who read all or part of the manuscript: Lorna Smedman, Gregory Masters, Rackstraw Downes, Joel Lewis, Cynthia Huntington, and Louise Hamlin. To those who talked about it with me and suggested ideas and poems: Bob Hershon, Donna Brook, Charles North, Christian McEwen, Chuck Wachtel, Patricia Spears Jones, Lucille Clifton, Cleopatra Mathis, Bill Cook, Grace Paley, Bob Nichols, Duncan Nichols, Anselm Berrigan, Steven Levine, Lewis Warsh, Ted Greenwald, Larry Zirlin. For consenting to be interviewed and for permission to quote from that conversation, Ron and Pat Padgett.

To Susan Bibeau, of the Dartmouth College Humanities Computing Center, who saved this manuscript from oblivion at least three times.

To LeAnn Fields, who saw the manuscript's possibilities before they were fully realized and remained steadfast despite scoffers; Allison Liefer, who was not only informative but encouraging; and Phil Pochoda, who invited me to send the manuscript to Michigan even though it's about poetry.

Grateful acknowledgment is made to the University of Iowa Press for permission to quote from *The Last Word: Letters between Marcia Nardi and William Carlos Williams*, edited by Elizabeth Murrie O'Neil (Iowa City, 1994); to Renée Weiss for permission to quote from *David Schubert: Works and Days*, published by Quarterly Review of Literature Poetry Book Series (Princeton, N.J., 1983); to Hanging Loose Press for permission to publish "Bible Stories" from *The Last Dust Storm* (Brooklyn, 1995) and "Two Helens" from *Borrowed Coats* (Brooklyn, 2001) by Wilma Elizabeth McDaniel; to *American Poetry Review* for permission to reprint "Caviar and Cabbage: The Voracious Appetite of Melvin Tolson," which appeared in the March–April 2000 issue; to Cliff Fyman, for permission to reprint "One Busy Busboy," which appeared in issue no. 5 of *Transfer* magazine; to Eileen Myles, for permission to reprint "On the Death of Robert Lowell" from *A Fresh Young Voice from the Plains* (Power Mad Press, 1981), and to quote from other works; and to Tracie Morris, for permission to reprint "Project Princess," which appeared in *Aloud: Voices from the Nuyorican Café* (Henry Holt and Company, 1994).

I've tried to acknowledge all other relevant texts that I read while researching this paper in the bibliography. I would, however, like to particularly acknowledge the inspiration and provocation of lectures and texts by Mary Childers, Sharon O'Dair, and the resplendent Tillie Olsen.

Contents

Introduction

"Distortion" or "Unexamined Factor"?

*I*n 1929, as Virginia Woolf prepared the lectures that would become her transforming book *A Room of One's Own,* she published an essay in the *Forum* titled "Women and Fiction." There Woolf writes that "it is in poetry that women's fiction is still weakest," and predicts that women will soon look beyond

> personal and political relationships to the wider questions which the poet tries to solve—of our destiny and the meaning of life. The basis of the poetic attitude is of course largely founded upon material things. It depends upon leisure, and a little money, and the chance which money and leisure give to observe impersonally and dispassionately. With money and leisure at their service, women will . . .write fewer novels, but better novels; and not novels only, but poetry and criticism and history. But in this, to be sure, one is looking ahead to that golden, that perhaps fabulous, age when women will have what has so long been denied them—leisure, and money, and a room to themselves. (84)

Woolf knew that writing required not merely pen and paper, but time to reflect and dream, freedom from intense deprivation, and the encouragement of a community of peers. It's impossible for me to read this paragraph without thinking of Jack London's *Martin Eden*, published twenty years before. The penniless young Eden writes his finest work at his sister's kitchen table, surrounded by family bustle and the anxieties of near-poverty, until his hard-working brother-in-law becomes impatient of the layabout's doodling and insists that he leave their house. Eden eventually becomes a successful novelist and can afford a mansion of his own. But he has been disappointed by the cynicism of publishing, the arrogance of the rich, the scorn and abuse endured when he was poor and unknown, the fawning and dissembling he encounters as celebrity. The prosperous Eden sinks into a depression that saps his will to write, and anticipating the tragic end of Hart Crane, he slips from the cabin of his ocean liner to disappear overboard.

There is no doubt but that London's hero had a huge working-class chip on his shoulder, which is why he must have appealed to Vladimir Mayakovsky. *Martin Eden* was one of Mayakovsky's favorite books. Unfortunately, no print of the Russian film version of the book, in which the poet played the title role, has survived. I doubt that you could see the movie in London in 1929. But did Woolf know of Mayakovsky and Jack London when she wrote, in "Women and Fiction," the following?

> In *Middlemarch* and *Jane Eyre* we are conscious not merely of the writer's character, as we are conscious of the character of Charles Dickens, but we are conscious of a woman's presence, of someone resenting the treatment of her sex and pleading for its rights. This brings into women's writing an element entirely absent from a man's, unless indeed he happens to be a working man or a negro, or who for some reason is conscious of a disability. It introduces a distortion and is frequently the cause of weakness. The desire to plead some personal cause or to make a character the mouthpiece of some personal discontent and

grievance always has a distressing effect, as if the point at which the reader's attention is directed were suddenly two-fold instead of single. (79–80)

Less than a century later, Woolf's position seems quaint. The twofold attention that she, in an echo of W. E. B. DuBois's "double-consciousness," laments as "distressing," appears nostalgically simple when compared to the multiplicities of self suggested by *The Invisible Man*, Robert Duncan's "The Self in Postmodern Poetry," or even Woolf's *Orlando*. The unity of character she applauds in the novels of the English masters strikes us as insensitive to its imperial, racial, gender, and class privileges. Besides religious fundamentalists, who now pretends to a single, undistorted view of reality? Tillie Olsen, an ardent admirer of Woolf, wrote in *Silences*, "No one has as yet written *A Room of One's Own* for writers other than women, still marginal in literature. Nor do any bibliographies exist for writers whose origins and circumstances are marginal. Class remains the greatest unexamined factor" (146).

Some things have improved since Woolf's essay, particularly for women with comfortable incomes who write poems, but also for men and women writers of color and from the lower class. Many things remain the same. Take Jed Rasula's *The American Poetry Wax Museum*, published in 1996 by the National Council of Teachers of English. Rasula claims that "the poetry world is now configured by four zones" (440). When he speaks of "the poetry world," he is really talking about the poetry scene in the United States, which he delineates into (1) the Associated Writing Programs; (2) the New Formalism; (3) language poetry, and (4) "various coalitions of interest-oriented or community-based poets" (440). This fourth (and, one would assume from the book, least significant) sector Rasula links to the "sixties counterculture," stressing the prominence of the black arts and women's movements. According to Rasula, while the identities of this last group of writers "have complex and nuanced theoretical significance, their writing has been nurtured in a nontheoretical and even anti-intellectual environment" (443). Thus even in Rasula's progressive criticism, women and poets of color continue to be stigmatized as "interest-oriented or community-based," perpetuating Woolf's distortion that artists from the dominant classes are not. But Rasula also perpetuates the myth that women and poets of color are largely anti-intellectuals, whose refusal to embrace the dominant poetic theories implies a lack of understanding or nuance in their writing. Pertinent to this book, Rasula dispenses entirely with the third arm of Woolf's analysis, that having to do with class.

Of course it's possible in the fluid class structure of the United States for a child of the working class to ascend the social ladder, to attend an elite university, and even to become a member of the AWP, New Formalist, or language "zones." Then, like Bill Clinton's, their careers will serve as reminders that no one in this country need bear forever the stigma of the "interest-oriented" or "community-based." Entry into the managerial class is now open on a limited basis even to women and people of color. So are considerations of class irrelevant to contemporary poetry, as a reading of Rasula might imply? Is a writer from the working class doomed to the resentments and distortions mentioned by Woolf? Can we see those "distortions" as something other than disability? While it's clear that most working-class Americans have a highly refined and discriminating sense of class distinctions (until recently my stepfather considered people who buy beer in bottles, instead of cans, as hoity-toity), why would we, well past the turn of the millennium, call attention to class at all, particularly as it manifests in an activity such as poetry that is by many considered marginal itself?

A couple of years ago, I sat on a panel at the St. Mark's Poetry Project discussing the workings of class in contemporary American poetry. The panel was overweighted with poets from working-class backgrounds. But then it is they, and not members of the upper classes, who are most eager to discuss the subject. I reluctantly accepted the invitation to address a subject I had thought about much, but not without worrying that I was being put back into an old box. The audience was more various in origin, but generally responded in two ways. Many took the occasion to stand up and declare themselves more working class than thou. When someone mentioned the name of a poet not in attendance, a panelist derided his working-class credentials: "Sure, he grew up in a working-class neighborhood, but his family owned the bar!" Others generally dismissed class differences as foreign to poetry, and praised instead the classless society that they had joined when they became poets.

Later, over drinks, some friends confided that they were disturbed by the us-versus-them tendency of the speakers. But to me the panel resembled a working-class family reunion: free-flowing laughter, voices on the edge of tears, sudden outbursts and angry recriminations, intermittent solidarity, vehement unreason, anecdotes freighted with self-pity—and beneath all, the bond of class loyalties. It was not pretty, but generated enough electricity to light a small town.

To speak about class in the United States, we must invent a way to do it that distinguishes our fluid situation from rigid European structures, but does not ignore that the most successful democratic movements in this country in the last fifty years (civil rights, feminism, gay and lesbian liberation) opened the managerial class and helped reduce discrimination within it, but failed to minimize the expanding gap between classes that has produced the most alarming, and burgeoning, symbol of class strife in America—the gated community.

In a television documentary, Henry Louis Gates Jr., William Julius Wilson, and Cornel West—all at the time members of Harvard University's African-American Studies Department—agreed that the gap between classes in the United States may now be greater than that between "races." As basketball star Charles Barkley reportedly replied when members of his family criticized him for supporting the Republican Party, "They don't understand that I'm rich now."

I have been fortunate to find many friends and acquaintances willing to talk about the intersection of class and poetry, both in person and through the library. To their queries about this book, I seldom had answers, only an admission that the vocabulary I lacked suggested territory for investigation. Robert Duncan found in Whitman "the informing principle at work in ideas of democracy, of faring forth where no lines are to be drawn between classes or occupations, between kinds of intelligence, between private and public, but daring the multitude of lives to be lived and seeking in each life its own individual potentialities" (*Fictive Certainties*, 203). That proposal was refined one rainy Vermont morning as I was speaking with Pat and Ron Padgett about the poet Ted Berrigan. Ron said that Ted and he

> didn't write poems honoring the dignity of the working man or the troubles of the working class. However, there are lots of things about our poetry that were formed by the class we came from. The very fact that Ted and I became poets and especially the kind of poets we became, that is, not traditional poets—we didn't write "The Cremation of Sam McGee"—ejected us from our class. So it's very interesting to have grown up in a certain class and still feel in many ways that it made you who you are, and yet know that you can never really be a part of it again because of your interest in art and writing. It's really weird. And one's writing continues to be influenced by—not only by the origins, but by the knowledge of the distance between you and

your origins. So it's not only the presence of the class, it's the absence of the class at the same time.

This book might have addressed the connection articulated by Marcia Nardi between "being stuck at the ribbon counter at Woolworth's for eight hours a day at the minimum hourly wage, and my inability to function as a poet!" But I'm a poet, not a sociologist. Instead of writing about poems that didn't get written, I write about a few that did. Though it's possible to read these poems without contemplating the complexities of social class, I hope something is gained by reading them within this context.

The "Uneducated Poets"
Stephen Duck and
Ann Yearsley

*I*n 1732, a London bookseller published an unauthorized volume of poems to which he gave the title, *Poems on several subjects/written by Stephen Duck, lately a poor thresher in a barn, in the county of Wilts, at the wages of four shillings and six-pence per week:; which were publickly read in the drawing-room at Windsor Castle, on Friday the 11th of September, 1730, to Her Majesty: who was thereupon most graciously pleased to take the author into her royal protection, by allotting him a salary of thirty pounds per annum, and a small house in Richmond in Surrey to live in, for the better support of himself and family.* The pensioned Duck complained about the piracy; he would have liked an opportunity to further revise the poems before publication.

In 1831, Robert Southey, then English poet laureate, published an introduction to a volume of "Attempts in Verse by an Old Servant," John Jones. This introduction was later expanded and published separately as *The Lives and Works of the Uneducated Poets*, with an eight-page list of subscribers consisting mostly of nobles and clerics. Among Southey's uneducated poets were the Thames waterman John Taylor; shoemaker James Woodhouse;

pipe-maker and trumpeter John Frederick Bryant; the "Bristol milkwoman," Ann Yearsley; and the "thresher-poet," Stephen Duck.

When J. S. Childers edited a new version of Southey's *Lives* another one hundred years later, he wrote that "probably no writer has ever disturbed the recognized *littérateurs* of his day as did Stephen Duck, who from being 'a poor thresher in a barn,' was, because of the favour of the Queen [Caroline], suddenly thrust into national fame." Jonathan Swift resented Duck's modest pension and complained strongly about it in letters to Pope and Gay. He was quick to deride the thresher in a characteristically cynical epigram.

> The thresher, Duck, could o'er the Queen prevail;
> The proverb says, no force against a flail.
> From threshing corn, he turns to thresh his brains,
> For which his Majesty allows him grains;
> Tho' 'tis confest, that those who ever saw
> His poems, think them all not worth a straw.
> Thrice happy Duck, employed in threshing stubble!
> Thy toil is lessen'd, and thy profits double.
>
> (Southey, 109)

In his own letter to Gay, Alexander Pope approved of the pension; he had met Duck and judged him "an honest man." But when Queen Caroline sent him Duck's manuscripts for comment, Pope remarked uncharitably that "most villages could supply verses of equal force." A contrary view was expressed by Horace Walpole fifty years later (November 13, 1784) in a letter to Hannah More: "When the late Queen patronized Stephen Duck, who was a wonder only at first, and had not genius enough to support the character he had promised, twenty artisans and labourers turned poets, and starved" (Southey, 183). Walpole's estimate may have been low. Inspired by the story of Duck's ample pension, a gaggle of brickmasons, carpenters, and other working men published manuscripts that failed to support Pope's judgment. Following Swift's example, a flurry of parodies also appeared, including *The Thresher's Miscellany*, which stated upon the title page that the author is "now a poor Thresher in the County of Suffolk, at the wages of Five Shillings and Six Pence per Week, though formerly an Eton Scholar" (Southey, 184).

What so riled and antagonized the English literary world of the 1730s? "The Thresher's Labour" was composed when Stephen Duck was twenty-five years old, supporting a wife and three children on the meager thresher's income announced on the title page of the pirated edition. As evidence that Duck deserved inclusion in *The Lives and Works of the Uneducated Poets*, Southey noted that Duck much admired Milton but read him with the aid of a dictionary, as "one would Latin and Greek"; that he was fond of Seneca and Epictetus but read them only in translation; and that he owned but one volume of Shakespeare that included only seven plays. Of course, Duck was also devoted to the *Spectator*, which he frequently took into the fields with him to read during work breaks. The *Spectator* published the most fashionable writers of the times, and today we might deem the combination of stylish coffeehouse prose, Latin philosophy, and the verse of Milton and Shakespeare sufficient education for a young poet, whether laborer or gentleman.

Even Duck's detractors admit the "charm and authenticity" of his most famous poem, and recognize its singularity as a "vividly realistic" portrait "from first-hand experience" of "the labourer's life." It is still included in anthologies of the era and can also be found in *The Penguin Book of English Pastoral Verse*, edited by John Barrell and John Bull, though under the heading "Some Versions of Anti-Pastoral," where it is grouped with poems by Goldsmith, Crabbe, and John Clare—all poets distinguished from the pastoral company chiefly by their more intimate acquaintance with village life.

The Birds salute us, as to Work we go,
And with new Life our Bosoms seem to glow.
On our right shoulder hangs the crooked Blade,
The Weapon destin'd to uncloath the Mead:
Our left supports the Whetstone, Scrip, and Beer;
This for our Scythes, and these ourselves to cheer.
And now the Field, design'd to try our Might,
At length appears, and meets our longing Sight.
The Grass and Ground we view with careful Eyes,
To see which way the best Advantage lies;
And, Hero-like, each claims the foremost Place.
At first our Labour seems a sportive Race:
With rapid Force our sharpen'd Blades we drive,
Strain ev'ry Nerve, and Blow for Blow we give.
All strive to vanquish, tho' the Victor gains
No other Glory, but the greatest Pains.

Admittedly, the poet's point of view is part of the poem's attraction.

Week after week, we this dull Task pursue,
Unless when winn'wing Days produce a new;
A new, indeed, but frequently a worse!
The Threshal yields but to the Master's Curse.
He counts the Bushels, counts how much a Day;
He swears we've idled half our Time away:
"Why, look ye, Rogues, d'ye think that this will do?
Your Neighbours thrash so much again as you."
Now in our Hands we wish our noisy Tools,
To drown the hated Names of Rogues and Fools.
But wanting these, we just like School-boys look,
When angry Masters view the blotted Book:
They cry, "their Ink was faulty, and their Pen;"
We, "the Corn threshes bad, 'twas cut too green."

The poem still sounds fresh and direct, and Duck brings a perspective to the literature found in none of his more famous con-

temporaries. His poem arrived at a time when the most respected poets looked to classical sources, particularly Virgil, and the favorite form was a pastoral in which rustics enamored with the greenery of their surroundings declaimed like English gentry. The rural setting of Duck's poem found a responsive audience in readers attracted to pastoral verse, while at the same time complicating the landscape with a farm laborer who actually spoke as a laborer—who grew sweaty, thirsty, fatigued, and resented his demanding boss.

> Nor yet, the tedious Labour to beguile,
> And make the passing Minutes sweetly smile,
> Can we, like Shepherds, tell a merry Tale;
> The Voice is lost, drown'd by the louder Flail.
> But we may think—Alas! what pleasing thing,
> Here, to the Mind, can the dull Fancy bring?
> Our Eye beholds no pleasing Object here,
> No chearful sound diverts our list'ning Ear.
> The Shepherd well may tune his Voice to sing,
> Inspir'd with all the Beauties of the Spring.
> No Fountains murmur here, no Lambkins play,
> No Linnets warble, and no Fields look gay.

His direct and economic diction bespeaks a sincerity and concision rare in an age of fussy ornament, extended metaphor, and stilted rhetoric. The realism in his verses was enough to inspire Crabbe a generation later to write in "The Village,"

> Yes, thus the Muses sing of happy swains,
> Because the Muses never knew their pains:
> They boast their peasants' pipes; but peasants now
> Resign their pipes and plod behind the plough;
> And few, amid the rural-tribe, have time
> To number syllables, and play with rhyme;
> Save honest *Duck*, what son of verse could share
> The poet's rapture and the peasant's care?

Or the great labours of a field degrade,
With the new peril of a poorer trade?

(Barrell and Bull, 400)

One account has it that Duck's wife strongly disapproved of his versifying, even complaining to neighbors and parish authorities that he was bedeviled, because he would frequently sit by himself counting on his fingers and mouthing rhymes. Unfortunately, this wife never enjoyed the rewards from his vocation; she died at about the same time that Queen Caroline discovered the thresher.

The queen put Duck on salary as keeper of her library at Richmond, called Merlin's Cave. She approved of the recent widower's marriage to one of her housekeepers, Sarah Big, and encouraged him to study for holy orders. He spent the rest of his life studying theology and Greek, and writing on order and to occasion the society verse that was the mode of the day. A quick and able student, Duck continued to rise in station, even as his verse "degenerated into conventional pastoral and artificial diction" (Drabble, 304). In 1746, at the age of forty-one, he was ordained a priest; in 1750, was made chaplain to a regiment of the Dragoon Guards; in 1751, became a preacher at Kew Chapel, and in 1752 obtained the parish of Byfleet in Surrey. This last appointment was contended by those who argued that Duck lacked sufficient Latin to be entrusted with such an office, but his royal patrons stood by his appointment.

Despite the success of Duck's career as poet, scholar, and clergyman, the modest introductions that he devised for later editions of his poems suggest he was embarrassed by the parodies and attacks upon him by the very poets whose company he sought to join. In *The Country and the City* Raymond Williams praised Duck's early poems for altering the English landscape by shifting point of view and particularizing the nature of rural labor. Williams added, however, that "within a few years Duck was writing, with the worst of them, his imitations from the classics, elevated and hollowed to the shapes of that fashionable culture which was not only a literary stance—the 'high' tradition—but, as always, a social ratification" (90). In the last years of his life he quit writing completely and in 1756 committed suicide by drowning.

The stratified society of eighteenth-century England allowed Duck to prosper, but never to sever the thresher from "thresher-poet." Likewise, Mary Leapor remained the "Kitchen maid of Weston," Mary Collier the "Washer-woman," and Ann Yearsley the "Bristol milkwoman." In each case the "uneducated poet" was esteemed not for the quality of her verse but the novelty of her origin, as if the mystery was that these creatures wrote poems at all. When their efforts were encouraged, it was as novelties, and it quickly turned to discouragement if there were any attempt to leap stations.

When Leapor's verses were published, Duck was among the list of subscribers. But unlike the fortunate Duck, Leapor failed to attract a rich patron, was dismissed from her position in the kitchen (possibly because of her writing), and returned home to keep house for her father, who didn't much care for the scribbling either. She survived at home for only several years before her early death.

Another contemporary of Duck's, Mary Collier, objected to the portrait of laboring rural women in these lines from "The Thresher's Labour":

> Our Master comes, and at his Heels a Throng
> Of prattling Females, arm'd with Rake and Prong;
> Prepar'd, whilst he is here, to make his Hay;
> Or, if he turns his Back, prepar'd to play:
> But here, or gone, sure of this Comfort still'
> Here's Company, so they may chat their Fill.

Ah! were their Hands so active as their Tongues,
How nimbly then would move the Rakes
    and Prongs!

From our vantage, the women's greater sense of community, their scorn for the master's authority, and their playfulness are wholly admirable. But Collier was eager to prove the women more hard-working and obedient than the men. She responded in 1739 with "The Woman's Labour," a poem that disputes the thresher's portrayal, while flattering the poet by imitation. The advertisement to the poem stated,

> Tho' She pretends not to the Genius of Mr. Duck, nor hopes to be taken Notice of by the Great, yet her Friends are of Opinion that the Novelty of a Washer-Woman's turning Poetess, will procure her some Readers. (Landry, 56)

As forecast, Collier did not gain a patron and apparently paid from her own earnings to publish her poem. Later in life, she complained that she had benefited little from it. She remained in her station, continuing to work as a washerwoman and brewer to employers who apparently little valued her verse.

Among other worker poets who gained public notice in the second half of the eighteenth century were two poets from Scotland, Janet Little and Robert Burns. Burns's origins would later endear him particularly to Walt Whitman. There was also Ann Yearsley, the "Bristol milkwoman."

Like Duck, Ann Yearsley was inspired by her reading of Milton and "a few plays" by Shakespeare. She also read Edward Young's *Night Thoughts* and Pope's *Eloisa to Abelard*. And her success depended largely on the acquisition of a patron. But in that patronage, she was not so fortunate as to be linked to a queen. Instead she was championed by the philanthropic Hannah More, whose cook first tipped her off to Yearsley's poetry. Apparently More went to check out Yearsley and was appalled by the conditions in which she was living. According to More's account, the Yearsley family (including her husband, six children, and Ann's mother) were dwelling in a stable, on the verge of starvation, and More's intercession was life-saving (for all, that is, except Yearsley's mother, who took ill and failed to recover). In the middle of this extreme poverty, More found "a Milker of Cows, and Feeder of Hogs, who has never even seen a dictionary" (Landry, 130), but who composed stunning "untutored" verses.

More may not be an entirely reliable witness about the extent of Yearsley's poverty or her education, but Yearsley was grateful for the aid she provided to the family. Yearsley responded by addressing a number of conventional verses to "Stella," the name she chose for More, from "Lactilla," her faithful milkmaid.

Yearsley was not born into the laboring class. Unlike Duck, Collier, or Leapor, the Yearsleys had begun married life as small property owners, and it's unclear how they fell into the stable where More found them. More speculated that it was a combination of the husband's stupidity and, on the part of the wife, that "poetic vice," a lack of thrift. In any case, there was no doubt that the Yearsleys had fallen on hard times. More, with the aid of her friend Elizabeth Montagu, established a subscription to publish a book of Yearsley's poems. Worried that the Yearsleys would mismanage the funds collected by the subscription, More was determined that Yearsley's literary success not disrupt her barnyard labors. It seems that Yearsley was destined to pay the price for Duck's example. More wrote to Lady Montagu, "I am utterly against taking her out of her Station. Stephen was an excellent Bard as a Thresher, but as the Court Poet, and Rival of Pope, detestable" (Landry, 20).

Without consulting Yearsley, More established a trust to support the poet and her children (her husband was to have no access to the money), with More and Montagu as trustees. She also published a preface to the first edition of Yearsley's poems in which she embarrassed Yearsley by describing the impoverished plight in which she found her and claiming to have corrected the "grossest" inaccuracies and offenses in the poet's primitive art.

When Yearsley attempted to negotiate terms of the trust so that she might be one of the trustees, More became indignant. In her letters she complains about "that wretched milkwoman."

> Prosperity is a great trial, and she could not stand it. I was afraid it would turn her head but I did not expect it would harden her heart. I contrive to take the same care of her pecuniary interests, and am bringing out a second edition of her poems. My conscience tells me I ought not to give up my trust for these poor children, on account of their mother's wickedness. (Waldron, 72)

Yearsley had a different version of the feud.

> Miss More appeared to be greatly moved, and told me imperiously, that I was a "savage"—that "my veracity agreed with my other virtues"—that I had "a reprobate mind, and was a bad woman."—I replied, that her accusations could never make me a bad woman—that she descended in calling me a savage, nor would she have had the temerity to do it, had I not given myself that name! (Landry, 152)

The timing of the incident was unfortunate for Yearsley. It was no longer the era of Queen Caroline, but the precipice before the French Revolution. The anxious English upper classes were not charmed by an ungrateful milkmaid poet who deemed herself the equal of her patrons. The determined Yearsley, however, self-published further editions of her poems, including *A Poem on the Inhumanity of the Slave Trade* (1788), *Stanzas of Woe* (1790), and *The Rural Lyre* (1796). In the reaction following the French terror, she composed sympathetic elegies for Louis XVI and Marie Antoinette. Mary Waldron's excellent biography of Yearsley assures us that she earned enough from her writings to open a circulating library and to apprentice her sons to reputable trades.

In *The Oxford Companion to English Literature*, one finds Stephen Duck cross-referenced to the entry "primitivism." As the *Oxford Companion* describes primitivism, it was

> an 18th century phenomenon that grew out of an interest in the educational and philosophic theories of Rousseau (and was) accompanied by great enthusiasm for travel writings and for real-life South Sea Islanders, Eskimos, Lapplanders, Negroes, etc. . . . Homegrown primitives were also in demand, and "peasant" poets such as Stephen Duck and Anne Yearsley (the Bristol milkwoman, who wrote pastoral verses to her patron Stella from her faithful Lactilla) were taken up by eager patrons.

The *Oxford* goes on to say that one of the most important figures in the movement was Thomas Gray, whose poems (especially *Elegy in a Country Churchyard*, with its nod to the "mute inglorious Miltons") "reflect his own feeling for the non-classical past and tend to connect poetic genius to liberty." The entry concludes: "It was in the cause of liberty that writers such as Cowper and Day defended the Noble Savage and attacked the slave trade. The ideas embodied in Primitivism were in many ways continued in the Romantic movement, with its stress on Nature, freedom, and the natural man."

In 1832, only a year after Southey's *Lives of the Uneducated Poets* appeared, the vagaries of the era before copyright allowed a translation of part of his book into American. The Boston firm of Perkins and Marvin published a *Biography of Self Taught Men* by B. B. Edwards that included, in addition to chapters on successful American businessmen and politicians such as Henry Clay, chapters on John Jones and Stephen Duck. Edwards lifted these chapters verbatim from Southey's book, except for the poetic excerpts, which were deleted. In crossing the Atlantic, Jones and Duck were transformed from "uneducated poets" to "self taught men." As a woman, Yearsley was excluded. Ideas about nature, freedom, and the natural man that were by then in

England associated with rebel Romantic poets were championed in the United States by prominent intellectuals such as Emerson and Margaret Fuller, and appealed to a people with the active confidence of enterprising pioneers and ambitious merchants. Though I have found no evidence that Walt Whitman saw the *Biography of Self Taught Men*, it typified the self-assertive spirit of the Jacksonian era and anticipated the calls of Young America to which he harkened.

A Song for Occupations
Whitman the Rough

Why what have you thought of yourself?
Is it you then that thought yourself less?
Is it you that thought the President greater than you? or
the rich better off than you? or the educated wiser than
you?
Because you are greasy or pimpled—or that you was once
drunk, or a thief, or diseased, or rheumatic, or a pros-
titute—or are so now—or from frivolity or impo-
tence—or that you are no scholar, and never saw your
name in print . . . do you give in that you are any less
immortal?

*W*hen Walt Whitman sent Ralph Waldo Emerson a copy of
the first edition of *Leaves of Grass*, he received in reply an enthusiastic letter that, without asking the author's permission, Whitman printed in the second (1856) edition of his book. Whitman
added his own rambling and self-promoting public response in
which he addressed Emerson as "Master." In this letter to Emerson, Whitman attacked the old class lines of Europe, and
declared that American poets refuse to be classed off.

Poets here, literats here, are to rest on organic different bases
from other countries; not a class set apart, circling only in the

circle of themselves, modest and pretty, desperately scratching for rhymes, pallid with white paper, shut off, aware of the old pictures and traditions of the race, but unaware of the actual race around them.

In his gracious letter, Emerson had applauded the "free & brave thought" of *Leaves of Grass*. He spent the summer praising the book to his Concord circle. Discouraged by their response, he wrote to Thomas Carlyle:

> One book, last summer, came out in New York, a nondescript monster which yet had terrible eyes and buffalo strength, and was indisputably American—which I thought to send you, but the book throve so badly with the few to whom I showed it, and wanted good morals so much, that I never did. Yet I believe now again, I shall. It is called *Leaves of Grass*,—was written and printed by a journeyman printer in Brooklyn, New York, named Walter Whitman; and after you have looked into it, if you think, as you may, that it is only an auctioneer's inventory of a warehouse, you can light your pipe with it. (363)

By the time Emerson read *Leaves of Grass*, Whitman was almost forty years old. He had taught school, edited newspapers in Brooklyn, Manhattan, and New Orleans, published a temperance novel, and for almost twenty years had been contributing short stories and articles to the same literary journals as Poe, Melville, and Hawthorne. Yet Emerson chose to identify him as "a journeyman printer." It's true that in the poem, Whitman chose to represent himself as a rough from the working class. The now familiar portrait of the author on the title page showed Whitman in informal dress, with open collar. But Emerson went out of his way to meet Whitman, visiting him in Brooklyn and dining with him twice. He also sent his friends to meet Whitman—including Thoreau, Bronson Alcott, and Moncure Conway. By the time he wrote to Carlyle, Emerson was no longer writing about a mysterious stranger. Identifying the author as a printer may have served him in the same way that identifying Duck as a thresher or Yearsley as a milkwoman served their patrons—giving him a way to approve of a book with "buffalo strength" but lacking the literary taste that would make it acceptable to his peers.

Only a year younger than Karl Marx, Whitman had the advantage over his European contemporary of immersion in the flexible class structure of antebellum boomtown New York. Whitman watched members of his family rise to comfortable middle-class status while others sank into poverty, despair, prostitution, and premature death. He himself bobbed up and down on an annual, sometimes daily, basis, as he bounced from journeyman printer to editor to bookseller to carpenter to real estate speculator to freelance journalist to volunteer nurse—and, in later life, from civil servant to unemployed poet to comfortable government sinecurist to dependent invalid to minor celebrity to impoverished but beloved old man. He had the wide experience to appreciate the material base of society, but aspired only to healthy roughneck living. Whitman appreciated money, but never cared to earn much of it, was careless and irresponsible, walked away from good money building houses to devote most of two years to writing the first edition of his little book, and when he did have money used it to attend Italian operas and buy gifts for his family and favorite young men.

The decades that formed Walt Whitman, the 1830s and 1840s, were years of rapid radical change in the United States, years of optimism and plunder. Looking back on the lawless genocidal policies of President Andrew Jackson toward Native Americans, it's difficult to recall that for many Americans, Jackson embodied the promises of liberty and equality only latent in the Declaration of Independence. A self-educated man from the Tennessee frontier, Jackson's contempt for the ethics, laws, and proprieties of Federalist merchants, judges, and bankers translated into an image of populist challenge to conservative institutions. As related in Alice Felt Tyler's *Freedom's Ferment* or even in a parody of reform such as Hawthorne's *Blithedale Romance*, the two decades were a time of utopian experiment and liberating promise. As a young journalist and man about Manhattan, Whitman was in the front row to gaze on every passing bandwagon. Often, he would swing aboard for a brief or extended ride. Whitman tempered the revolutionary patriotism and class consciousness of his carpenter father with the embracing generosity of his Quaker mother. He added to that stew his own infatuation with the rough B'hoys of the Bowery.

> Through me many long dumb voices,
> Voices of the interminable generations of slaves,
> Voices of prostitutes and of deformed persons,
> Voices of the diseased and despairing, and of thieves and
>   dwarfs,
> Voices of cycles of preparation and accretion,
> And of the threads that connect the stars—and of wombs, and
>   of the fatherstuff,
> And of the rights of them the others are down upon,
> Of the trivial and flat and foolish and despised,
> Of fog in the air and beetles rolling balls of dung.

Among Whitman's journalistic assignments, he was directed by the *New York Evening Post* in 1851 to review an exhibition of paintings at the Brooklyn Art Union. He was particularly charmed by Walter Libbey's picture of "a handsome, healthy country boy" playing a flute.

> He has a brown wool hat, ornamented with a feather; rolled-up shirt sleeves, a flowing red cravat on his neck, and a narrow leather belt buckled round his waist. . . . Abroad, a similar subject would show the boy as handsome, perhaps, but he would be a young boor, and nothing more. The stamp of class is, in this way, upon all the fine scenes of the European painters . . . while in this boy of Walter Libbey's, there is nothing to prevent his

becoming a President, or even an editor of a leading newspaper. (*Uncollected Poetry and Prose*, 237–38)

Or even a Homer of the masses?

The time that it took Whitman to write and ready for publication the first edition of *Leaves of Grass* remains conjectural. The best guess has only fragments preceding 1854. In any case, 1855–56 were years of intense, inspired composition. The first edition of 1855 was followed by another edition just a year later that included twenty new poems plus revisions to many of the twelve that appeared in the first. Among the poems written that year were "A Woman Waits for Me," "Spontaneous Me," "Respondez," and those that would eventually be titled "This Compost," "Salut au Monde," "To a Foiled European Revolutionnaire," "By Blue Ontario's Shore," "Crossing Brooklyn Ferry," and "Song of the Open Road."

These years were also the most eventful of Whitman's New York literary career, effectively ended with his move to Washington during the Civil War. This was the time of his most frequent visits to Pfaff's, the underground saloon at Bleecker and Broadway that was the hangout for New York bohemia. It's at Pfaff's that Whitman became close with Henry Clapp, translator of the socialist Fourier, author of the free-love tract *Husband vs. Wife*, and editor of the *Saturday Press*, a popular magazine that regularly printed Whitman's poems and was one of the staunchest promoters of *Leaves of Grass*. Among other frequenters of Pfaff's with whom Whitman struck up friendships were Ada Clare (the "Queen of Bohemia" and unmarried mother of a son whose father was composer Louis Moreau Gottschalk), the actress Adah Isaacs Menken (notorious as the "Naked Lady" of Broadway, she was at this time married to a heavyweight boxing champion), the humorist Artemus Ward, the young careerist William Dean Howells, and many other prominent writers and journalists whose reputations failed to outlive them. When Whitman was not at Pfaff's, he was a frequent guest at the house of his friend Mrs. Abby Price, a writer and lecturer in the antislavery, women's rights, and dress reform causes. The Price household included a Swedenborgian boarder, with whom Whitman spent many hours talking about spiritual matters.

During this time of intense poetic composition, Whitman also wrote an exposé, "The Slave Trade—Fitting Out Vessels in the Port of New York," that appeared in the August 2, 1856, edition of *Life Illustrated.* Though the trade had been outlawed for half a century, Whitman claimed that it flourished openly from the port of New York, with law officials failing to enforce the statutes and maybe even conspiring to profit from it. He wrote that within the previous three years, eighteen slave ships had sailed from the port. Yet since 1845, there had been few arrests for violating the ban—and no convictions. Whitman's contempt for slavery and those who defended it was ardent and explicit. Never was that contempt more forcefully expressed than in the essay he wrote that summer attacking the "three hundred and fifty thousand" slave masters who were nefariously undermining democracy in a nation of thirty million.

The Eighteenth Presidency remains Whitman's most angry class-conscious prose. The author set his fiery essay in type, printed proofs, and offered the stereotypes free to any publisher or "rich individual" who would distribute it. Yet it remained in proofs during Whitman's lifetime and has seldom been reprinted since. Perhaps the author was too critical of the major political parties and the delegates to their conventions; perhaps his open call to American workers was considered too class-volatile. It's not in Mark Van Doren's *The Portable Walt Whitman* or James E. Miller Jr.'s *Complete Poetry and Selected Prose*, the standard classroom editions for most of the last fifty years. Nor is it included in Gary Schmidgall's selected Whitman. Justin

Kaplan's Library of America *Complete Poetry and Collected Prose* does include it, tucked at the back of the book among "Supplementary Prose."

Directed to young workmen in all parts of the country, *The Eighteenth Presidency* is a screed against the presidential candidates nominated by the major party conventions that year, James Buchanan and Millard Fillmore, whom Whitman derides as servants to slave masters. But Whitman begins the essay with a brief lesson on class, comparing the class divisions of old Europe to the theoretical classlessness of the United States. The American theory has not been realized, however, and Whitman complains that the practice of a few politicians representing the richest interests more closely resembles old ruling notions. He is incredulous.

> Are lawyers, dough-faces, and the three hundred and fifty thousand owners of slaves, to sponge the mastership of thirty millions? Where is the real America?

The Eighteenth Presidency veers from buoyant celebratory catalogs of Americans at work and play to savage denunciations of the cynical politicians who exploit the good nature and endless energy of these "sturdy American freemen." The stunning juxtapositions of patriotic praise and desperate outrage are consonant with the contradictions that charge Whitman's poems from this period. The essay is inflamed by the same poetic and political heat that fires the early *Leaves,* and has an urgency missing from Whitman's later, more reflective prose. Whatever the virtues of his other compositions, at no other time in his life does he write with such fire, and surely not this savage humor. For example, this Swiftian list of delegates to the major party conventions of 1856:

WHO ARE THEY PERSONALLY?

Office-holders, office-seekers, robbers, pimps, exclusives, malignants, conspirators, murderers, fancy-men, post-masters, custom-house clerks, contractors, kept-editors, spaniels well-trained to carry and fetch, jobbers, infidels, disunionists, terror-ists, mail-riflers, slave-catchers, pushers of slavery, creatures of the President, creatures of would-be Presidents, spies, blowers, electioneers, body-snatchers, bawlers, bribers, compromisers, runaways, lobbyers, sponges, ruined sports, expelled gamblers, policy backers, monte-dealers, duelists, carriers of concealed weapons, blind men, deaf men, pimpled men, scarred inside with the vile disorder, gaudy outside with gold chains made from the people's money and harlot's money twisted together; crawling, serpentine men, the lousy combings and born freedom sellers of the earth. (*Complete Poetry*, ed. Kaplan, 1313–14)

Whitman insists "that Washington, Jefferson, Madison, and all the great Presidents and primal warriors and sages were declared abolitionists." He proposes "One or Two Radical Parts of the American Theory of Government":

> Man can not hold property in man. . . . Every rational uncrimi-nal person, twenty-one years old, should be eligible to vote, on actual residence, no other requirement needed. . . . The whole American government is in itself simply a compact with each individual . . . to protect each one's life, liberty, industry, acqui-sitions, without excepting one single individual out of the whole number, and without making ignominious distinctions. This is government sublime; this is equal; otherwise it is a government of castes, on exactly the same principles with the kingdoms of Europe. (1320)

The Eighteenth Presidency is charged by partisan Old Testa-ment–like prophecies, call-and-response bursts of headline jour-nalese and brisk brute paragraphs, and vigorously uncharacteris-tic satiric darts. Among Whitman's poems, only "Respondez" manifests the same angry disillusion. And among his poems, only "Respondez" has shared the same sort of publishing his-tory. Though Whitman included it in the 1856 edition of *Leaves*, it provoked such angry attack that Whitman deleted most of the poem from later editions, keeping only its ghostly echoes in "Reversals" and "Transpositions."

> Let all the men of These States stand aside for a few
>   smouchers! let the few seize on what they choose! let the
>   rest gawk, giggle, starve, obey!
> Let shadows be furnish'd with genitals! let substances be
>   deprived of their genitals!
> Let there be wealthy and immense cities—but still through any
>   of them, not a single poet, savior, knower, lover!
> Let the infidels of These States laugh all faith away!
> If one man be found who has faith, let the rest set upon him!
> . . . .
> Let a man seek pleasure everywhere except in himself!
> Let a woman seek pleasure everywhere except in herself!
> (What real happiness have you had one single hour through
>   your whole life?)
>
> (*Complete Poetry*, ed. Miller, 396–97)

The manic chockablock invention that characterizes the 1856 edition of *Leaves* and *The Eighteenth Presidency* will find no analog in American poetry until *Howl* is published a century later. Whitman emerged from the Civil War mellowed by his service to the hospitalized and fatigued by the illness that he suffered near the war's end. But the courage and good nature of his wounded boys pledged him more than ever to America's new democratic era, and he would continue to discourse on the same obsessive themes in *Specimen Days* and *Democratic Vistas*. Never again, however, would he write with the urgent ecstatic edge that characterizes the poems and prose of 1855–56.

> Let the people sprawl with yearning aimless hands! Let their
>   tongues be broken! Let their eyes be discouraged! Let none
>   descend into their hearts with the fresh lusciousness of
>   love! . . .

Let the theory of America still be management, caste,
  comparison! (Say! what other theory would you?)
Let them that distrust birth and death lead the rest! (Say! why
  shall they not lead you?)
Let the crust of hell be neared and trod on! Let the days be
  darker than the nights! Let slumber bring less slumber than
  waking-time brings!
Let the world never appear to him or her for whom it was all
  made!

(Complete Poetry, ed. Miller, 395)

By the time he published *November Boughs* thirty years later
(1887), democracy was still much on Whitman's mind, but he
was more likely to draw prudent distinctions between the greatness of art and its political implications. In an essay on Shakespeare, but especially in essays on Carlyle and Tennyson, he was
willing to forgive, even appreciate, an antidemocratic bias.

> The course of progressive politics (democracy) is so certain and
> resistless, not only in America but in Europe, that we can well
> afford the warning calls, threats, checks, neutralizings, in imagi-
> native literature, or any department, of such deep-sounding and
> high-soaring voices as Carlyle's or Tennyson's. (*Complete Poetry,*
> ed. Kaplan, 1163)

His reminiscences of these English authors accord them the
judicious respect he pays in his later writings to conservative,
respectable American peers such as Longfellow and Lowell. But
if you are looking for affection, you must turn to his much
longer essay on the Scot ploughboy, Robert Burns. He admits
that Burns has "little or no spirituality," and that he gives
"melodies, and now and then the simplest and sweetest ones; but
harmonies, complications, oratorios in words, never." But he
calls Burns "in some respects, the most interesting personality
among singers," and finds in his songs special qualities to endear
him to Americans. After assessing from some critical distance

the successes and limits of Burns's poems, the aged Whitman admits that his own favorites are those indelicate ditties often censored from popular editions.

> [Burns] treats fresh, often coarse, natural occurrences, loves, persons, not like many new and some old poets in a genteel style of gilt and china, or at second or third removes, but in their own born atmosphere, laughter, sweat, unction. . . . Is there not something in the very neglect, unfinish, careless nudity, slovenly hiatus, coming from intrinsic genius, and not "put on," that secretly pleases the soul more than the wrought and re-wrought polish of the most perfect verse? (1159)

Though the trials of American expansion and Gilded Age corruption caused Whitman's faith in democracy occasionally to waver, by the end of his life he was proclaiming with greater zeal than ever the ability of a new, classless American literature to hearten the common people of all lands. In *A Backward Glance o'er Travel'd Roads*, he writes,

> Of the great poems receiv'd from abroad and from the ages, and to-day enveloping and penetrating America, is there one that is consistent with these United States, or essentially applicable to them as they are and are to be? Is there one whose underlying basis is not a denial and insult to democracy? . . . [T]he Old World has had the poems of myths, fictions, feudalism, conquest, caste, dynastic wars, and splendid exceptional characters and affairs, which have been great; but the New World needs the poems of realities and science and of the democratic average and basic equality, which shall be greater. In the centre of all, and object of all, stands the Human Being, towards whose heroic and spiritual evolution poems and everything directly or indirectly tend, Old World or New. (*Complete Poetry*, ed. Kaplan, 663–64)

> Without yielding an inch the working-man and working-woman were to be in my pages from first to last. The ranges of

heroism and loftiness with which Greek and feudal poets endow'd their god-like or lordly born characters—indeed prouder and better based and with fuller ranges than those—I was to endow the democratic averages of America. (*Complete Poetry*, ed. Kaplan, 668)

In the prefaces Whitman composed in 1887 for the English editions of *Specimen Days*, Whitman summarized for European readers the "reason-for-being" of his books.

[I]n the volume, as below any page of mine, anywhere, ever remains, for seen or unseen basis-phrase, GOOD-WILL BETWEEN THE COMMON PEOPLE OF ALL NATIONS. (1193)

And in the preface to the English edition of *Democratic Vistas*, published the following year, he continued to proclaim that the "great test or trial case" of America "means, at least, eligibility to Enlightenment, Democracy, and Fair-show for the bulk, the common people of all civilized nations" (1195).

When the psalm sings instead of the singer,
When the script preaches instead of the preacher,
When the pulpit descends and goes instead of the carver that
    carved the supporting desk,
When the sacred vessels or the bits of the eucharist, or the lath
    and plast, procreate as effectually as the young silversmiths
    or bakers, or the masons in their overalls,
When a university course convinces like a slumbering woman
    and child convince,
When the minted gold in the vault smiles like the
    nightwatchman's daughter,
When warrantee deeds loafe in chairs opposite and are my
    friendly companions,
I intend to reach them my hand and make as much of them as I
    do of men and women.

"Poor Doc, Nobody Wants His Life or His Verses"
W. C. Williams and *The New Masses*

*W*riting from London in 1917, T. S. Eliot dismissed a critic's notion that *Leaves of Grass* might have influenced Ezra Pound, and used the occasion to attack free verse. Although not yet thirty and a resident of England for less than ten years, Eliot was already a parody of the "tory and a high church and state man" that Whitman warned Americans about in an essay on Sir Walter Scott. Eliot's position was absolute: "*Vers libre* does not exist. . . . [I]t is a battle-cry of freedom, and there is no freedom in art" (32).

Also writing from London, Pound took a more balanced position:

> I think one should write vers libre only when one "must," that is to say, only when the "thing" builds up a rhythm more beautiful than that of set metres, or more real, more a part of the emotion of the "thing," more germane, intimate, interpretative than the measure of regular accentual verse; a rhythm which discontents one with set iambic or set anapaestic. (12)

He commented, "Perhaps a few good poems have come from the new method, and if so it is justified" (3).

Back in the United States, William Carlos Williams approached the same subject in an essay titled "America, Whitman, and the Art of Poetry" that appeared in the *Poetry Journal*. At thirty-four years old, Williams was just beginning to hit his stride as modernist. Only four years before, the exhibition of modern paintings at the Armory in New York City had inspired a drastic change in the way he composed poems. Since then, he had moved from Keatsian imitations and sonnets with stanzas like the following:

> I've fond anticipation of a day
> O'erfilled with pure diversion presently,
> For I must read a lady poesy
> The while we glide by many a leafy bay

to the stark currency of *Al Que Quiere*, which includes poems of defining Williams style (e.g., "Danse Russe," "Portrait of a Woman in Bed," and "January Morning").

> Though the operation was postponed
> I saw the tall probationers
> in their tan uniforms
> > hurrying to breakfast!

He was writing with the radiant confidence that comes with the first blush of artistic maturity. In some ways, the rest of his writing life would consist of attempts to return to the clarities of this first liberation. And the attitudes and contradictions that would define his career had already come to center stage. He began his essay by proclaiming, "Whitman created the art in America" (1), and continued, "We cannot advance until we have grasped Whitman and then built upon him" (2). He admitted that Eliot and Stevens "are going over the forms of yesterday and making fine stuff to read and enjoy" (4), but several lines later changed his mind and accused Eliot of "timorously reverting to popular forms" (4). Though he concedes the point about no art being truly free, even calls free verse a "misnomer," he suddenly reverses field on that too:

> And yet American verse of today must have a certain quality of freedom, must be "free verse" in a sense. It must be new verse, in a new conscious form. But even more than that it must be free in that it is free to include all temperaments, all phases of our environment, physical as well as spiritual, mental and moral. It must be truly democratic, truly free for all. (2)

This inclusive democratic faith distinguishes him from most leading poets of his generation, and provides the continuing basis of his antipathy to Eliot in particular. As is clear from this early essay, Williams always paid attention to the publications of Eliot, Stevens, Pound, and especially Marianne Moore. But to consider him in that company limits and distorts our view. Williams chose to stand beside another sort of poet. He expressed it best in 1946, after reading Arthur Schlesinger Jr.'s *The Age of Jackson*, and being particularly impressed by Schlesinger's chapters on Jacksonian democracy as intellectual movement and on its connection to literature. At last he found the words to clarify the difference between his aesthetic and that of his old friend and nemesis Pound. Williams described Pound's as the "classic attitude," that the greatness of the past must be translated into present terms by poets in intimate contact with the Great Minds. But Williams insists there is another source of inspiration,

> the present, from the hurly-burly of political encounters which determine or may determine it, direct. This is definitely not the academic approach to literature. It is diametrically opposed to the mind to mind fertilization of the classical concept. Whereas the academic approach may speak *about* us always in the forms of

the past or their present day analogues, the direct approach *is* the spectacle of our lives today, raised if possible to the quality of great expression by the invention of poetry.

. . . The forms of the past, no matter how cultivated, will inevitably carry over from the past much of the social, political and economic complextion of the past. And I insist that those who cling basically to those forms wish in their hearts for political, social and economic autocracy. They think in terms of the direct descent of great minds, they do not think in terms of genius arising from great movements of the people—or the degeneracy of the people, as known in the past. ("Letter to an Australian Editor," 10)

For Williams, poetic invention cannot be disentangled from the circumstances of its generation. Like Whitman, he sees its genius "arising from great movements of the people." Though he insists that the poet is *not* a politician, but an artist, "the poet's very life but also his forms originate in the political, social and economic maelstrom on which he rides" (11). The difficulty and precision of the distinction he draws between the poet who rides the maelstrom and the poet who becomes a politician may be assessed by the paths of his friends, most of whom either removed themselves to an aestheticism apart from the fray, or succumbed to the brutalities of partisan doxy.

The last half of "America, Whitman, and the Art of Poetry" is given entirely to a survey of the poetry magazines of the day. Thirteen are named and assessed by the sorts of poetry they publish. Though his personal fondness for Pound is evident, even in 1917 Williams distances himself from Pound's proselytizing. As he casts about the poetic landscape, he approves wholly only Marianne Moore and Carl Sandburg. The magazines *Poetry, Soil, Others,* and *Seven Arts* receive praise, but except for *Others* (to which Williams contributed poems and money) that praise is qualified. He describes *Seven Arts* as "made for middle-aged, semi-brave revolutionists who have fixed their canons of taste beyond question" (4), and *Poetry* as "so amiable that it has made amiability almost a virtue" (3). About *The Masses: A Monthly Magazine Devoted to the Interests of the Working People*, he wrote, "*The Masses* cares little for poetry unless it has some beer stenches upon it" (4).

Paul Mariani's excellent biography of Williams might easily have been subtitled "A career in the little magazines." Has the publishing history of any other canonized poet of the twentieth century been so widely or intensely involved with novice and ephemeral publishers? In his *Autobiography*, Williams wrote,

> The little magazine is something I have always fostered; for without it, I myself would have been early silenced. To me it is one magazine, not several. It is a continuous magazine, the only one I know with an absolute freedom of editorial policy and a succession of proprietorships that follows a democratic rule. There is absolutely no dominating policy permitting anyone to dictate anything. . . . I have wanted to see established some central or sectional agency which would recognize, and where possible, support little magazines. I was wrong. It must be a person who does it, a person, a fallible person, subject to devotions and accidents. (266)

At present "outsider art" is much discussed, but seldom has anyone stated the case for it as lucidly as Williams. In his life, he moved from magazine to magazine, group to group, often publishing simultaneously in magazines at contrary ends of the political and social spectrum. Part of this owed to his irritable restlessness, part to his generous open nature, part to his inability to find sufficient outlets for his copious production. But part must also owe to Williams's aesthetic faith, which consisted largely of his commitment to the "hurly-burly" of the democratic maelstrom.

During the Jazz Age (and Prohibition), it was relatively easy for Williams to maintain the progressive modernist position he attributes to Whitman, Sandburg, and Moore, and remain comfortable among the contributors of almost any magazine that would have him. During that time of individual liberation and relative prosperity, avant-garde art and leftist politics coexisted happily in America's little magazines, where experiments with poetic line or bohemian gestures were deliciously naughty but unthreatening. As a doctor whose practice tended mostly to working-class and immigrant families, Williams witnessed first-hand the widening gap between the country's rich and poor, a gap obscured for many writers by the prosperity of the era. But as the events in Communist Russia spurred a repressive domestic backlash, Williams championed the poor and persecuted almost as ardently as he did modernism. Yet he was also a prosperous professional and family man from the suburbs, accustomed to comforts that included extended trips to Europe, where he sent his children to school. It's not surprising to discover that he worked on behalf of the Democratic Party in his town and served on his local school board. Unlike many of his alienated peers, Williams practiced politics on the level at which most decisions that directly affect the neighborhood are made.

In 1926 he published a story titled "The Five Dollar Guy" in *New Masses*, the revived version of the magazine that was interested only in poetry with "some beer stenches upon it." A woman patient had told him a story about the manager of the local oil business, who so regularly propositioned the neighborhood's working-class housewives that they referred to him as "the five dollar guy." When Williams submitted this class-conscious story to *New Masses*, a magazine that called, "Sit down, you bricklayers, miners, dishwashers, clothing workers, harvest hands, cooks, brakemen, and stone-cutters . . . Write us the truth—it is more interesting than most fiction" (Klein, 78), he gave them too much truth. He had forgotten to change the name of the oil business and was sued for fifteen thousand dollars, which at that time amounted to three years of his income. For a nerve-wracking few months, Williams worried that the case would go to trial, where an adroit lawyer for the plaintiff might easily sway jurors by exploiting the fact that the story appeared in a Communist magazine! He eagerly settled the suit for five thousand dollars and an agreement never to publish the story again. Fortunately, that was also the year that Marianne Moore obtained for him the Dial Award, a prize of two thousand dollars that helped him to defray his expenses.

Had it not been suppressed by the libel suit, "The Five Dollar Guy" would have fit nicely among the short stories in *The Knife of the Times*, published in 1932. About them, Williams told Edith Heal,

> I was impressed by the picture of the times, depression years, the plight of the poor. I felt it very vividly. I felt furious at the country for its lack of progressive ideas. I felt as if I were a radical without being a radical. The plight of the poor in a rich country, I wrote it down as I saw it. The times—that was the knife that was killing them. (*I Wanted to Write a Poem*, 49)

As depression-era politics became increasingly polarized, Williams's furious radical sympathies inspired him to print often in *New Masses* and other Communist or fellow-traveling magazines, such as Jack Conroy's *Anvil*, which eventually became the *Partisan Review*. But "without being a radical," his position in these magazines was tenuous and not entirely welcome. The editors and many other contributors were struggling to define a territory for proletarian art, and as that territory became more contested, the political hard-liners reacted vehemently against avant-garde modernism. Williams was among those caught in the middle, trying to reconcile what he considered a progressive, pragmatic poetics with progressive, pragmatic politics.

On the first page of the October 1930 "John Reed" issue of *New Masses*, Mike Gold printed a letter addressed to him by Ezra Pound defending Mussolini's "co-operative state" from the "bawling" of the proletariat and attacking the "damnable features of Xtianity [that] still show their hebrew origins." After acknowledging Pound as "a writer's writer; one of those craftsmen and pioneers because of whose restless experiments lesser men often rise to popularity," Gold went on at length to challenge Pound, Eliot, and the other American literary exiles who had embraced Fascism. Williams liked this issue so much that he responded immediately with a contribution to the magazine and a note that ended, "I'm for you, I'll help as I can. I'd like to see you [the magazine] live. And here's to the light, from wherever it may come." Characteristically, however, Williams also admitted his reservations.

> The only thing is, what the hell? I feel in a false position. How can I be a Communist, being what I am. Poetry is the thing which has the hardest hold on me in my daily experiences. But I cannot, without an impossible wrench of my understanding, turn it into a force directed toward one end, Vote the Communist Ticket, or work for the world revolution. There are too many difficulties, unresolved difficulties in my way. I can however see the monumental blockwit of social injustice surrounding me on every side. But why they arise, God only knows. But in any case they are there and I would give my life freely if I could right them. But who the hell wants my life? Nobody as far as I can see. They don't even want my verse, which is of more importance.

It was a strange chord to strike in a magazine committed to proletarian art. Williams's letter was printed with others that began, "Cut out those highbrow articles on Humanism and other intellectual junk"; "Cut your book section in half. Give us more on the class struggle"; and "I wish there were more proletarian fiction." The editors published Williams's letter under the mocking title "Poor Doc, Nobody Wants His Life or His Verses."

Between 1932 and 1942, in addition to continuing his busy medical practice, Williams published three books of poems, two books of stories, an opera libretto, and the novel *White Mule*. He collaborated with Fred R. Miller on an unfinished novel about an African American jazz musician, and with Nathanael West edited several numbers of the revived magazine *Contact*. He also found time to read and review a revealing succession of younger poets, among them George Oppen, Muriel Rukeyser, Sol Funaroff, Norman MacLeod, Kenneth Patchen, and Marcia Nardi. Though Funaroff, MacLeod, and Nardi no longer are as widely read as Oppen, Rukeyser, and Patchen, there is a coherence about this group of poets and the work they were writing during that decade that illustrates and reinforces persistent thematic and formal concerns in William's own poems and fiction. Some were Communists, some aggressively working-class. The poetry of all of them shone a hard light on the inequities of American capitalism.

More surprising, however, was the doctor's enthusiasm for a Missouri farmhand poet named H. H. Lewis, about whom he wrote three essays in two years. The last of these he deemed so important that he was willing to compromise his own principles about freedom of association in order to get it published.

Between 1930 and 1935 Lewis published four "cheaply printed, paper-covered" pamphlets of poetry that sold for ten cents each and were advertised regularly in the *New Masses*. Williams was enamored of the format, claiming that "Given cheap books—if the purveying of them can be solved also—there will be in fact a renaissance" (Breslin, 76). The titles express forcefully the tone and substance of Lewis's political commitment: *Red Renaissance, Thinking of Russia, Salvation,* and *Road to*

Utterly. Williams's first review of them, published in *Poetry*, concluded:

> This isn't Auden or Spender. This is a Missouri farmhand, first cousin to a mule, at one dollar a day. If Lewis' subject matter should distress some readers, it's about time they learned what makes their fruits and vegetables come to ripeness for them—and what kind of thoughts their cultivation breeds in a man of revolutionary inheritance. (*Something to Say*, 69)

Perhaps Williams felt he was not given sufficient space in *Poetry* to finish with Lewis; perhaps he felt that magazine the wrong venue for his review. For he was intent on publishing a longer review of the pamphlets in the *New Masses*. But Williams also published in the *Partisan Review*, and in 1936 the magazines were locked in Trotskyite-Stalinist combat, with neither interested in a united front. The editors at the *New Masses*, supporters of Stalin's Russia, told Williams that he could no longer publish with them if he continued to publish in the *Partisan Review*. Williams was so eager to publish his essay on Lewis with the former that he didn't hesitate. He informed the *PR* editors of the ultimatum and admitted he had decided to stick with the *New Masses*.

What did Williams so admire in H. H. Lewis? First there was the dime format, which he considered an innovation in poetry publishing. He was also impressed by the "one positive thing" Lewis had learned from the modernism of the first quarter of the century, his use of dialect. Lewis wrote with the "confidence and the natural ease of a native speaking his own language as he hears it spoken in his own place and day" (*Something to Say*, 80). Williams praised Lewis's "direct interest" in current politics. "He speaks directly, and so automatically does away with the putrescence of symbolism with which the first quarter of the century was cursed" (81). And he seemed pleased to declare that "there is here no question of high art." He admitted the derivative nature of Lewis's forms, copied from "anything from Gray to Whitman, including the books of limericks, nursery rhymes, popular songs, Poe—anything you please, even back to Shakespeare—he'll borrow the form and turn it to his own purpose" (80). He noted that the "four booklets show little or no progress in form. . . . If anything, I think the earlier ones are better, more forthright, cruder with a more patently outraged conscience. Lewis has let go, seeming to be repeating himself" (82).

This stern judgment of Lewis's formal laxity is characteristic. The other reviews of young poets that Williams wrote during this time (cf. Oppen, Rukeyser, or Funaroff) continually address formal difficulties, which makes Williams's willingness to overlook Lewis's redundant or derivative form the more startling. Suddenly and anomalously, Williams turns from the formal concerns of the contemporary poem to a more pressing poetic (and political) matter.

> Without saying that Lewis is important as a poet, which is a point that will have to be very carefully considered before a proper opinion can be arrived at, I will say that he is tremendously important in the United States as an instigator to thought about what poetry can and cannot do to us today. He speaks in no uncertain terms. He speaks with fervor, a revolutionary singleness and intensity of purpose, a clearly expressed content. He knows what he wants to say; he is convinced of its importance to a fanatical degree. . . . There is a lock, stock, and barrel identity between Lewis today, fighting to free himself from a class enslavement which torments his body with lice and cow dung, and the persecuted colonist of early American tradition. (77)

Lewis's poems were "pure American revolutionary stuff. . . .There is no one that as directly expresses the mind of the United States as Lewis does now." But when it came to supporting these claims with evidence, this is what Williams offers as a moment when "the charge [of Lewis's poems] is so great that it lifts the commonplace to lyric achievement":

> Russia, Russia, righting wrong
> Russia, Russia, Russia!
> That unified one sovereign throng,
> That hundred and sixty million strong,—
> Russia!
> America's loud EXAMPLE-SONG,
> Russia, Russia, Russia!

Unable to imagine the circumstances that would convince anyone of these verses, I tracked down copies of Lewis's pamphlets; these lines were not untypical. Nor were these, about which Williams said that the poet's "convictions have forced him to write well":

> I'll say,
> Phew, for Chrissake,
> The brains of the "Brain Trust," that's it,
> Rrrrrotten!
>
> Pity the poor American donkey,
> Pity the poor American farmhand,
> The one nervously zigzagging,
> The other compelled to jerk him back to the row,
> Plowing under cotton!
> Such an "asinine"
> Torturing
> Strain on the sound sense of both!
>
> *(Something to Say,* 81)

To end the *New Masses* essay, Williams revised the final paragraph of the *Poetry* essay quoted above. The later version reads:

> If Lewis' subject matter should distress some readers, it's about time they learned what makes their fruit and vegetables grow for

them, what kind of thoughts their cultivation breeds in a man, and, finally, what the meaning of poetry is. (82)

In the years that Williams was championing H. H. Lewis, his old friend Ezra Pound was writing *Jefferson and/or Mussolini*. They were contesting heritage to the American revolutionary spirit—Williams found it embodied in a Missouri farmhand who wrote communist doggerel, Pound in Il Duce, the "Boss" of Fascist Italy. It was a time when many felt they had to choose sides between laborer or boss. Williams believed that Lewis had "one great strength without which there can be no art at all—the sincerity of belief in his own songs, in their value, and in their power to penetrate to the very bones of the listeners." Maybe Pound believed the same about Mussolini. Sincerity is a virtue that cries for context.

In *Writing the Radical Center: William Carlos Williams, John Dewey, and American Cultural Politics*, John Beck persuasively argues that Williams's political position during this period resembled the philosopher's. Though opposed to the injustices of industrial capitalism, their faith in civil liberties and the individual imagination made both men wary of Communism. Given, however, the particular issues and battles of the era, they often found themselves in sympathy with Communist figures and positions. Beck concludes that, like other American liberals such as Dewey, Herbert Croly, or Randolph Bourne, Williams's commitment to a sense of community prevented him from developing any clear analysis of or position on class conflict. Ultimately, he was an ameliorist, not a revolutionary.

Though Williams wrote again for the *New Masses* and was ardently anti-Franco during the Spanish Civil War, after the Lewis articles his writings move back toward an emphasis on technique. It is not a political turning, as *The Wedge* and "The Pink Church" later demonstrate, but an aesthetic distancing, as if the outbreak of war moves him to emphasize tolerance and inclusion instead of partisan rigor. By 1940 he wrote in a letter to *Furioso:*

> Pound says that everything he's written has economic implications. Everything (nearly) that Genevieve Taggard writes says "better read Marx." In other words most of the modern poets *think* they're pointing toward something which they believe is right. And I want to know if they've picked the right medium. (*Something to Say*, 105)

Special Handling
David Schubert and
Marcia Nardi

When you cannot go further
It is time to go back and wrest
Out of failure some
Thing shining.

> (From David Schubert's "No Finis")

How difficult the erection of even
That fence of a hair's breadth
Between
Body and soul of another,
Whose presence crams
Ten worlds:
Like trying to keep entirely to the right
Or to the left, jostled,
On a city pavement;
Or on a country lane,
When letting a car pass,
Having
One foot upon grass
And another on gravel.

> (From Marcia Nardi's "Poem")

*A*spiring poets from the lower class are often discouraged. If they are hardy as Whitman, they may disregard the "foo-foos" and prevail. If they are too fragile, they may withdraw from the fray, cease writing altogether. In between, they persist, complaining frequently about their lack of literary acquaintance or distaste for the business that accompanies their craft. David Schubert and Marcia Nardi complained frequently about their lack of publishing success, bemoaned their ineptitude at self-promotion, and voiced discomfort when they made rare ventures among "literary people." Schubert's wife insisted that his inability to get his poems published sapped his confidence in his gift and provoked the episodes that forced his institutionalization for the final three years of his life before his early death at thirty-three. The querulous Nardi alienated almost everyone who was ever close to her, but attributed her unbearable loneliness primarily to a lack of intelligent literary friends—a lack she explained by her background, not her personality. Both were damaged humans who harbored special talents, talents lauded by readers as disparate as William Carlos Williams, John Ashbery, Frank O'Hara, Louise Bogan, Theodore Weiss, and Morton Dauwen Zabel. Both were convinced—or deluded—that more propitious circumstances would have allowed their poetic talents to thrive.

John Ashbery's book *Other Traditions* includes essays on Schubert and five other poets, each of whom, he says, "requires some kind of special handling. That is, reading their work isn't quite as simple as it is with a poet such as, say, John Keats, where one can simply take down a book from a shelf, open it, and begin reading and enjoying it. With each of them, some previous adjustment or tuning is required. It also helps to know something of their biographies and the circumstances in which they worked, since these are responsible for wide fluctuations in the quality of what they wrote" (95).

Urging James Laughlin to publish Nardi's poems, William Carlos Williams wrote: "She asked me not to plead for her, wants the verses to speak for themselves. I told her she needed a push, that her work did not appeal at first glance since its virtue was not on the surface of it—no matter how good a critic might pick it up. The form is nil but there are lines and passages that are worth all the facile metrical arrangement ever invented and these do actually give the verse a form of its own" (O'Neil, 26).

What form of special handling is required to appreciate the poems of David Schubert or Marcia Nardi?

Born in unpromising circumstances, both were traumatized in childhood, handicapped by poverty, and alienated from Whitman's "average." As adults, they were abusive to their intimates, helpless and inept in practical matters, fumbling in promoting their poems. They suffered chronic illness, sometimes self-exacerbated, and spent great amounts of time in the care of doctors, occasionally in institutions.

Yet John Ashbery wrote that he values the poetry of David Schubert "more than Pound or Eliot" (122). After he compared the experience of reading Schubert's poems to opening a window in a stuffy room, he was bemused to discover that William Carlos Williams had used the same metaphor to describe reading Schubert's poetry forty years before.

Williams was willing to say publicly that "Marcia Nardi, here and there in her work, produces a line or two as fine as anything that anyone, man or woman, writing today can boast of" (414). Upon receiving a later batch of poems, he wrote to her that "they strike completely through my guard, they appear to me to be among the best poems of the day—so much better than what is being accepted as good that I feel ashamed for my sex, to say the least, which generally monopolizes the scene. They are warm, defenseless, and well made" (O'Neil, 140).

David Schubert was born in 1913 in New York City to working-class parents who soon moved to Detroit. He was one of three children. When he was twelve, his father abandoned the family, his mother committed suicide, and it was David who discovered her body. The children were sent to live with relatives, which brought David back to Brooklyn. In the biographical note he compiled for the only publication of a substantial group of his poems during his lifetime, he wrote that he "was homeless from the age of 15, supporting himself by selling newspapers, working as busboy, soda jerker, waiter, farm hand and various other jobs. At one time he did a turn in the C.C.C. All in all, it was anything but an easy life" (*Five Young American Poets*, 134). Yet somehow he distinguished himself enough at Boys High in Brooklyn to obtain a scholarship to Amherst College.

At Amherst he was inspired to pursue poetry but wasn't engaged with other classes. He gained the attention of Robert Frost and John Theobald, but lost his scholarship. Frost and other professors interceded on his behalf, and Schubert was allowed to return to college, but he lasted less than a semester. He spent the next couple of years in the Civilian Conservation Corps and as itinerant farm laborer, often sleeping in missions and shelters. He also fell in love and at the age of twenty married Judith Ehre, a teacher at a progressive school in Manhattan. He and his wife found an apartment in Brooklyn Heights near where, Schubert was pleased to note, Hart Crane lived while composing *The Bridge*. They were friends with poets Ben Belitt, Horace Gregory, Marya Zaturenska, Theodore Weiss, and painter Mark Rothko. And in 1936, Schubert won a prize from *Poetry* magazine for his poem "Kind Valentine."

After this modest initial success, however, Schubert spent the remainder of the depression doing editorial work at the Brooklyn Institute of Arts and Sciences, reliant on his wife's income to support the household, and growing increasingly frustrated and disturbed by his inability to find a publisher for his poems. He was not idle. During the next ten years he composed a book of poems and a novel, completed undergraduate study at CCNY, pursued a master's degree in literature at Columbia, and then a second degree at Columbia in library science. His wife thought that in the Brooklyn Institute "David had a perfect job . . . for writing. But he did not want to work. He wanted money and he wanted to be at home and he wanted to write . . . as if that was *all* he wanted to live for" ("David Schubert," 250).

Schubert sought constantly for ways to leave his job. He hoped first that a master's degree would get him a college teaching gig, then hoped for a position in a college library, but finally returned to the Brooklyn Institute with promise of a "more responsible position."

> I am fired from my job by flames, big
> As angry consciences: I can do
> Nothing: I have not one ability! This man
> Whom I am waiting to see in the lobby—
> All my life I am waiting for something that
> Does not eventuate—will he
> Exist?
>
> (From *Midston House*)

All the while, Schubert suffered from depression. His behavior became increasingly erratic and sometimes violent. His wife complained that he disappeared for days at a time without explanation. He was granted a month at Yaddo, but returned home after a mere three days. His wife wrote to Karen Horney, who couldn't see them but put the Schuberts in touch with another doctor. Schubert continued to see a psychiatrist, but wrote to a friend in 1940 that "the desert years seem to cling to me more and more. Every once in a while I think I'm out of it, but there are so many places in each day in which one falls onto nothing at all. But I'm making a battle with the Enemy, anyway" ("David Schubert," 209).

> Outside the window it was
> A hot saggy day in August. The Coast Guard
> Drilling at war, far as the Pacific.
> As poverty is my taskmaster, as

I study the Victor Record Catalog instead
Of listening to the paragon's
Prerogative: Eugene Ormandy, my
       Expectancy
Makes me slightly sick, as when years ago,
Hungry for food, I came to friends and they
Talked; now I wait for her to speak
The meanings which I must negate before
I am admitted to the gayest person.
     (From "Victor Record Catalog")

In early 1941 David admitted to Judith that he was having an affair with a coworker at the institute. Apparently she was having an affair too. They still enjoyed warm at-home evenings with friends, but these could erupt suddenly into abusive outbursts, even physical attacks. David finished a novel and tried to place it, but without success. As it returned from publisher after publisher, he became increasingly distraught. Enraged after one rejection, he destroyed the manuscript. That summer, New Directions decided to include Schubert's forty-page poetry manuscript, "The Simple Scale," in *Five Young American Poets: Second Series, 1941.* (The other four young poets were Paul Goodman, Jeanne McGahey, Clark Mills, and Karl Shapiro.) He received an advance of twenty-five dollars and wrote for the volume "A Short Essay on Poetry."

> What I see as poetry is a sample of the human scene, its incurably acute melancholia redeemed only by affection. This sample of endurance is innocent and gay: the music of vowel and consonant is the happy-go-lucky echo of time itself. Without this music there is simply no poem. It borrows further gayety by contrast with the burden it carries—for this exquisite lilt, this dance of sound, must be married to a responsible intelligence before there can occur the poem. Naturally, they are one: meanings and music, metaphor and thought. In the course of poetry's career, perhaps new awarenesses are discovered, really new

awarenesses and not verbal combinations brought together in any old way. This rather unimportant novelty is sometimes a play of possibility and sometimes a genuinely new insight: like *Tristram Shandy*, they add something to this Fragment of Life.

(*Five Young American Poets*, 136)

But by the time the book was published, he was again without a job. His note to close friends Theodore and Renée Weiss began, "Buy the book. I don't have no money, don't have no job, don't have nothin" ("David Schubert," 251). Judith said that he was "shattered" by the book's failure to attract reviews. By July, he was again contemplating abandoning writing.

A ghastly ordeal it was. In
Retrospect, I am no longer young.
Wise, sad, as unhappy as seeing
Someone you love, with whom life has
Brought suffering, or someone you
Have nothing in common with, yet love—
Unable to speak a word.

If when I say this I weep, it is not
Because my heart has turned into a
Lachrymose commentator; the
Discus thrower's still
There—the shining one, quick. It is because
In my moment of rejoicing, I
Thought that one who has suffered with me shall
Rejoice. There was no
One. Not one answered.

Of suffering, who wants to be reminded?

(From *No Title*)

But he returned to library school and by the following July had received a note from Morton Zabel suggesting he submit a manuscript for a competition in which Zabel was to be one of the judges. Schubert replied that he had a manuscript that he would like to have published, in part to be rid of it so he could begin upon another book, "a sort of Vita Nuova, strictly poetry" ("David Schubert," 265). But in January 1943, David grabbed a pair of scissors and threatened to kill Judith. She escaped from the apartment and returned the next morning with his psychiatrist.

> Bedlam was what we found; both windows were still open, the bed unslept in, torn pieces of David's manuscript lying about the floor, two oil paintings of me ripped out of their frames, were cut and scattered about, and things from drawers and closets were strewn everywhere. David was gone—and I felt, for the first time, relieved. ("David Schubert," 267)

Almost two weeks later, Judith received word that Schubert was in a mental hospital in Washington, D.C., where he had gone to see Archibald MacLeish about getting into the navy. Although David complained that his "acquaintance with literary people is rather limited" (227), Judith was able to call on Morton Zabel, Ben Belitt, and Louise Bogan for assistance in getting David transferred to Bloomingdale's in White Plains, New York, where he was diagnosed as paranoid schizophrenic ("David Schubert," 278–84; Ashbery, 128) and treated with electric shocks. He lived until April 1, 1946, when he died of tuberculosis while institutionalized in Central Islip, but only left the hospital for a brief period in late 1944, when his sister took him into her house. Shortly thereafter, however, he was found talking and gesticulating to himself in a New York City subway, and was again institutionalized.

For fifteen years after Schubert's death Judith, though remarried, and Theodore and Renée Weiss continued to offer his poems to publishers, until in 1961 Macmillan published his only book, *Initial A.* After another twenty-two years, the *Quarterly Review of Literature*, edited by the Weisses, published a special volume entitled "David Schubert: Works and Days."

Farewell, O zinnias, tall as teetotalers,
And thou, proud petunias, pastel windows of joy,
Also to you, noble tree trunks, by name
Elm, with your dark bark in the dark rain, couchant
Like comfortable elephants. And you
Mailbox colored robin's egg blue on the poor
House, shy, set back (a poor gentleman but
Irreproachable), with your shutters robin's egg
Green. You, street, striated with rain like a new penny,
And houses planted by arbor-vitae trees,
By miniature pines that lean against you for
Support—Hail and farewell!

(From *The Happy Traveller*)

As William Carlos Williams described his first meeting with Marcia Nardi, a "pint-size, bedraggled to the point of a Salvation Army reject" was "blown into my office one night, soaked to the skin by a heavy rain and in frightened need, in desperate need" (O'Neil, 161–62). She had traveled by ferry and train from her apartment in Greenwich Village to Rutherford, New Jersey, then walked in a torrent from the train station to Dr. Williams's office. A neighbor had phoned police during a violent shouting match between Nardi and her fifteen-year-old son. When Nardi told police that she could not control her son and that his school had recommended a psychiatric evaluation, they committed the boy to Bellevue. Now a repentant Nardi was eager to get him out. She was then involved with Harvey Breit, an editor at the *New York Times Book Review* and an acquaintance of Williams. It was apparently Breit who suggested that she visit Rutherford. Williams listened to her tale and offered counsel about getting the boy released. Before she left, Nardi handed the doctor a group of her poems and asked him to read them.

Not that I hoped the kind sense would reclaim
A heart in exile,

But flame at least conceals
The nature of its fuel:
Flame that steals
A shape no different
Nor hue nor name
From fragrant pine
Than from the rotting beams
Of tenements,
A beauty similar
From kindled forests
And the measured hearth.

Williams returned Nardi's poems with a brief letter in which he noted that "these poems have in them definitely some of the best writing by a woman (or by anyone else) I have seen in years. They also have plenty of bad writing in them, unfinished, awkward writing" (O'Neil, 9). He asked her to send him clean copies of the poems and to allow him to "work on them from time to time. . . . If you care to accept my criticisms that will be your responsibility. A valuable book may come of them in the end" (9). Thus began a correspondence that, though intermittent, extended for over fifteen years, and from which Williams extracted the "Cress letters" that he included in *Paterson*.

Marcia Nardi was born Lillian Massell in Boston in 1901. She attended Wellesley College, but left before graduation and moved to New York City. She described her immigrant family as "the worst kind of white trash" (O'Neil, 10) and apparently changed her name so they could not track her to New York. There she began a literary career that included early publications of poems and reviews in V. F. Calverton's *Modern Quarterly*, the *Nation*, *Literary Digest*, and the *New York Herald Tribune Book Review*. She met other young writers and artists and for a while lived in the same boarding house as Hart Crane and Allen Tate.

Her life changed profoundly after her son was born in 1926. Her relationship with the child's father ended soon after, and though she continued to publish poems during the next few years, as she raised the boy and tried to support him on a single income, she drifted away from writing. Between the years of 1929 and 1941, she published nothing while working at a series of jobs ranging from editing to waitressing to clerking in a five and dime. She was proud that, despite the depression, she did well enough to pay tuition for her son at private schools. By 1939 she began to write poems again, but "had to spend almost a year evolving all over again the very fashion of writing with which I'd left off, so that during the first year of my recent return to poetry, my work was almost as bad as that I'd written at 17 and 18, and had to undergo the very same processes of experimentation and development all over again before eventually growing into a continuity with the point where I'd previously stopped" (O'Neil, 12).

Sometime after beginning to write poems again, she began seeing Breit. Her first literary friend in many years, Breit encouraged her to submit poems for publication. Whether from timidity or indifference, she didn't. But she did feel strongly enough about them to take them with her when Breit arranged her appointment with Dr. Williams.

At that time she and her teenage son were sharing a one-room apartment on West Twelfth Street, though she was planning to send him to live with a farm family as soon as school was out. Williams promised to help her get her poems published and to find a suitable job. It's evident through the years of their correspondence that he prioritized his aid in that order. Nardi was grateful for his enthusiasm for her poetry. As she grew older and realized minimal publishing success, that enthusiasm became more important to her; she carried one letter from him in her pocketbook for years, folded so many times that she had to tape it together. But initially, she was less interested in his promotion of her poetry than in his concern for her welfare—and his friendship. She complained to Williams that "most of the people

I've had to associate with during my adult life have been either on the mental level of grocery clerks or else of the gutter" (O'Neil, 10). Though she met Williams only twice, he represented all that was missing in her life—artistic company, emotional intimacy, financial security. She was also chronically ill, perhaps hypochondriacal, racing from doctor to doctor without satisfaction and certain that only Dr. Williams would provide an accurate diagnosis. She believed that he was "the only man I've ever met who could have offered me the sort of relationship in which I could be completely contained" (O'Neil,191). As her letters became more effusive, revelatory, and desperate, his letters remained formal and increasingly distant, signed simply "Sincerely, W. C. Williams." He consistently addresses the business at hand, whether publishing, job hunting, or her mysterious illness, and advises her early in their correspondence that he would like to incorporate excerpts from her letters in the long poem he is writing.

But he steadfastly rebuffed her efforts to see him—apparently they met only once after her initial visit to his office, when he agreed to meet her at a midtown restaurant for dinner. Yet, because of his enthusiasm for her poems, he continued to intercede on her behalf. In response to her pleas of poverty, he frequently sent her "loans," though it's clear that neither of them expected that these would be repaid. He inquired about jobs and frequently sent her leads, often giving her the names of contacts and allowing her to use his name as reference. Most important from his view, he pushed James Laughlin to publish her poems, first in the *New Directions* annual, then in a small book.

This ain't no ingenue and she ain't dumb. . . . I wish I could do something for her, an unknown and unwanted . . . she's a good piece of steel. (O'Neil, 23)

It's very difficult to get the good out of her work. Very few people will stop to refine, in the judgments so poor an ore. That has been her life and it is palpable in everything she does. . . . I think the woman is wrapping up in the shoddy of her miserable existence a flash of real merit. (O'Neil, 37)

When Laughlin agreed to publish a group of seventeen poems in *New Directions* with an introduction by Williams, Nardi was initially excited—until she read Williams's introduction.

Marcia Nardi, now in her early thirties, is that woman you remember who disappointed her shocked parents by insisting on art school rather than college—and came to grief because of it. . . . She is that woman who got a job in the office of The Liberal Weekly, did a few reviews, spoke out of turn a few times and found herself working on tables in a cheap restaurant. Her feet and her hands bothered her. She's the one who was given the review to do, needing some extra cash, of a book by the editor's wife—and nobody told her why she was expected to praise it. . . . Marcia Nardi, here and there in her work, produces a line or two as fine as anything that anyone, man or woman, writing today can boast of. . . . There are lines, I claim nothing else, in that rubble that can have come from nothing other than a fine mind, courage and an emotional force of exceptional power. (*ND Seven*, 413–14)

Nardi resented Williams's special pleading—and patronizing tone. To Williams she wrote, "it embarrassed me, that preface, because in my private struggles and problems I prefer to live anonymously" (O'Neil, 76).

Instead of becoming angry with Williams, however, she became more demanding of his assistance at the very time that Williams was growing exasperated at her inability to find work despite the wartime economy's demand for labor. Though Nardi constantly complained about her impoverished circumstances and voiced a desire for "any secure regular income at all" (O'Neil, 104), she was unwilling to return to the kinds of unfulfilling jobs she had held for many years. She wanted more than an income.

My great handicap in living (and therefore in writing) has been for a long long time, not my consuming job and financial problems, and not my educational limitations, and not even my emotional frustrations, but only and entirely my lack of any connecting links whatsoever between the operative and inner aspects of my existence—combined with my lack of any intellectual companionship at all from one year to another. . . . *[N]o* mind can thrive when continually locked in upon itself—especially when it has never experienced (as mine never has) any of those beneficial "influences" in its formative years which play such an important part in the development of people who come from educated families. (O'Neil, 92–93)

This letter went on for eight pages. Near the end she made "a request which I hesitate to make and at the same time must. Will you let me spend an hour or so with you some time very soon— anywhere and any time (I could arrange that for your convenience)?" (O'Neil, 98). She would bring to the meeting for discussion "one or two very short poems" and maybe "a paragraph or two of prose." She also wanted to talk with him about "one particularly puzzling aspect of my health difficulties" which she suspected may "have psychological roots."

Apart from those very specific things that I should like so much to talk to you about (those to do with writing being more important to me than the other) I have been almost obsessed with the feeling for at least two weeks now, that this deadness of my mental faculties which I cannot seem to dispel, would immediately vanish if I found myself for an hour or so in the presence of someone whose own mind had a great deal of reality for me— and whose personality too of course since one cannot possibly sever the two. . . . [I]f you can possibly see your way to granting that request I make of you, it would mean a million times more to me than anything you could possibly do for me in purely practical ways—regarding jobs, et cetera. . . . If I should hear from you that you can and will let me see you some time soon, the mere prospect of that, I think, would snatch me into life. (O'Neil, 99)

After receiving no reply from the wary Williams, two weeks later she sent a three-page letter pleading for him to "come to [her] rescue" (O'Neil, 106). When he still did not reply, ten days later she wrote that she failed to understand what "would cause one person to turn a completely deaf ear to some really urgent life-or-death request of another person" (106) and pleading again that he meet her "for a short while" (107).

Three days after this third letter, she received the following brief note.

> My dear Marcia Nardi:
>   Though I have tried to find work for you I have not succeeded, under present circumstances my best advice would be for you to apply to one of the Federal Employment Bureaus and let them instruct you.
>   There's nothing more that I can do or say. This brings our correspondence to a close as far as I am concerned.
>   Yours very truly
>   W. C. Williams

Six years later Williams would write about Nardi, "I helped her for a while but found it was too much for me and withdrew after the first year or so" (O'Neil, 162). But she was not yet done with him. Determined to have the "last word" in their correspondence, within the next few weeks Nardi sent Williams three long indignant letters—and one postcard apprising him that she would continue to use his name as a job reference. Williams never answered the letters, but extracted long sections to use in *Paterson*.

Williams claimed that while readying *Paterson* for publication he tried to get in touch with Nardi to obtain written permission to use her letters in his poem. By that time, however, Nardi had moved to the country near Woodstock, New York, with John Lang, a painter and short-story writer. She had changed apartments so frequently while in the city, often leaving no forwarding address, that she could not be tracked through the post office. According to Williams, when he finally contacted her family, they asked him if he knew where she was. But in 1949, six years after her last letter to Williams, Nardi came upon the first two books of *Paterson* in a bookstore. When she found her letters within, she immediately wrote to the author to request copies of the books. She told him she was now married, but still impoverished, and suffering from liver and gall bladder troubles. In addition to the books, she told him she could also use "a couple of hundred dollars," help getting reviewing jobs, maybe a Guggenheim.

Williams replied promptly this time, promising to send books immediately and to "do what I can to come to your rescue" (O'Neil, 137). Though he couldn't send her "two hundred dollars in an offhand way," he enclosed twenty dollars as "token of my good will and appreciation for your assistance to me in the past. You've had plenty to contend with and I must say I admire your courage and persistence. No use going further into detail" (138). Williams, recalling the cost in settling the libel suit for "The Five Dollar Guy" twenty years before, might have worried about the legal ramifications of using Nardi's letters without written permission. He sent both Nardi's letter and a copy of his reply to his publisher, James Laughlin.

With this shaky start began another correspondence between Nardi and Williams that endured for six years. Nardi soon followed her first letter by sending Williams a group of poems written since they had last been in touch. Williams thought them "the best you have ever written," and with renewed enthusiasm for her talents, for the first time in their correspondence addressed Nardi as "Marcia" and signed himself "Bill." Over the next six years, he championed her poetry, sent her money, put her in contact with others who might help her, tried to get her into Yaddo, and eventually recommended her successfully for a Guggenheim. She responded with letters that chronicled her illness, romantic problems, poverty, and harsh social resentments—but whenever her correspondent seemed to be growing weary or cross with her, she could always woo him back with poems.

> How the rich move softly
> Through their injustices,
> Softly as the uncut grasses on summer noons they move—
> That tinkle? It's their cocktail glasses,
> That sound of hatchet blows?
> I do not know,
> For all is interstices
> And open meadowland and willow laces
> To their very gentle wickednesses
> That knuckleless as summer breezes go.
>
> (From "How the Rich Move Softly," *Poems*, 33)

Alan Swallow Press finally published a book of Nardi's poems in 1956, but it received little critical attention. The forty-page volume failed to include most of the twenty-two poems published in the New Directions selections of 1942 and 1947, nor any of the poems Nardi wrote before 1942. After this publication, Nardi enjoyed a modest career. In addition to her Guggenheim, she attended the Yaddo and MacDowell colonies and published occasionally in magazines, her last publication being a poem in the *New Yorker* in 1971. But her difficult personality continued to estrange acquaintances; she so harshly and publicly criticized fellow residents at Yaddo and MacDowell that she wore out her welcome at both colonies. In 1968 her son, then forty-two years old, told her he would have no more to do with her unless she would reveal to him his father's name. She refused and, though she lived another twenty years, never saw her son again. In late life she returned to Cambridge, Massachusetts, where she felt isolated from New York and the literary life she identified with it, and gained an unhappy reputation as a local eccentric. She spent her last years in a nursing home, to which she was tracked by Elizabeth Murrie O'Neil, who edited the volume of letters between Nardi and Williams at the heart of this account. She died in 1990.

WEIGHTED WITH LACK

My mind said *giddy-up* all day
But only time moved
Only time went away
The dray
Horse of my nothingness
Stayed.

Though morning and noon and the whole afternoon
To my *giddy-up* galloped away,
Weighted with lack—
The void in my loins
Overloading its back,
It did not go
It did not stir
It only strove and strained,
And the sun went down
And the wind blew
While I remembered the *whoa*
Of long ago
When light with having,
Of time and the wind and all things
I was the flow.

(*Poems*, 19)

Caviar and Cabbage
The Voracious Appetite of Melvin Tolson

> Countee Cullen and Langston Hughes represent the
> antipodes of the Harlem Renaissance. The former is a
> classicist and conservative; the latter, an experimentalist
> and radical. . . . With a biography that reads like a page
> from the Arabian Nights, Langston Hughes, the idealistic
> wanderer and defender of the proletariat, is the most
> glamorous figure in Negro literature.

So Melvin Tolson began the essay on Langston Hughes in his
master's thesis, "The Harlem Group of Negro Writers." The
glamour of Hughes's career contrasted starkly with Tolson's
own circumstances, supporting a wife and four children on the
modest income of an English teacher at a small black college in
East Texas. Yet Tolson knew something about Harlem, which
would remain at the center of his poetry for more than thirty
years.

> Alfred Kreymborg says of Langston Hughes: "He is the poet
> laureate of Upper Seventh Avenue." Of course, Mr. Kreymborg,
> not being a native of Harlem, got his streets confused. Seventh
> Avenue is the promenade of the upper classes and the strivers.

However, we know what Mr. Kreymborg means. Langston Hughes is the chief ballad-singer of proletarian Upper Lenox Avenue, the street of "the unperfumed drifters and workers" . . . Hughes has received much adverse criticism from the colored bourgeoisie. . . . They say his poems are "just like the nigger Blues," unmindful that this is the highest tribute they can pay to these artistic creations. ("Harlem Group," 120–28)

The son of a poor Missouri Methodist preacher, Melvin Tolson had earned money for college by working in a Kansas City meatpacking plant. He was recommended to Fisk University as a scholarship student, and after a year there moved on to Lincoln University, where he supplemented his scholarship over summer breaks by working as a waiter in Atlantic City hotels. While at Lincoln, he met Ruth Southall; they were married during his junior year. At graduation, the best job offer he received was from Wiley, a small black college in Marshall, Texas. He remained on the Wiley faculty for twenty-five years, raising a family of three boys and one girl, all of whom would receive advanced academic degrees. As coach of the Wiley debating team, Tolson developed a system that resulted in a ten-year winning streak, including a national championship win over the University of Southern California. But when Arna Bontemps visited Wiley at Tolson's invitation in 1941, he wrote to Langston Hughes that he was "amazed by the poverty" of the college. He added that some "of the top teachers were in patches" (Nichols, 76).

In addition to training champion debaters to compete on the national level, Tolson devoted much of the depression era to organizing sharecroppers in East Texas and Arkansas. (Tolson would note thirty years later that he had known Ralph Ellison, since both were active sympathizers, if not members, of the Communist Party during this time.) Because of the dangers of this activity, he was secretive about specifics, even with his family. His children recalled that he often returned from all-night meetings at dawn, but never said a word about where he had been. It was only through the stories recounted by those who accompanied him on those trips that they gradually realized how close he had come on several occasions to being lynched. From this vantage, it's difficult to judge which was most perilous—organizing sharecroppers or traveling through the Jim Crow South with a team of proud young African American debaters. Members of his teams (including the young James Farmer, later director of the Congress of Racial Equality) told many stories about narrow escapes from grave peril, both owing to and despite the qualities of Coach Tolson.

From 1937 to 1944 he also wrote a column for the *Washington Tribune* titled "Caviar and Cabbage." Reading those columns, it's apparent that Tolson made no distinction between the radical injunctions of Christ to give all that you have to the poor and Marx's "unto each according to need." But he was always careful to distinguish the teachings of Christ from the "mouth-Christianity" that dominated established churches, and the insights of Marx from the oppressions of the "Red Whites." Tolson consistently hammered "the Big Boys" whose limitless greed promoted colonialism in most of the world and racism in the United States. He stated frequently that the cause of racism was capitalism, the profits of which required an exploited low-wage class. Though his columns ranged far and wide, he returned most often to the politics of race, class, radical Christianity—and literature.

In the academic year 1931–32, Tolson's wife and four children moved in with his parents while he studied for a master's degree in comparative literature at Columbia University. That year in New York City researching "The Harlem Group of Negro Writers" inspired his first book of poems. Though the collection was only published posthumously, many of the poems from *A Gallery of Harlem Portraits* were published individually, beginning in 1937, when Tolson was thirty-nine years old.

Radicals, prizefighters, actors and deacons,
Beggars, politicians, professors and redcaps,
Bulldikers, Babbitts, racketeers and jig-chasers,
Harlots, crapshooters, workers and pink-chasers,
Artists, dicties, Pullman porters and messiahs . . .
The Curator has hung the likenesses of all
In *A Gallery of Harlem Portraits.*

(*Gallery of Harlem Portraits,* 4)

Because of this late beginning, although Tolson was as old as
the younger members of the Harlem Renaissance group (e.g.,
Hughes, Cullen), he was generally considered as a younger poet.
When Margaret Walker in 1950 wrote an article for *Phylon* magazine titled "New Poets of the Forties," she included Tolson
with herself in the third generation of Negro poets, following
that of the Harlem Renaissance and the protest poets of the
1930s (e.g., Sterling Brown and Frank M. Davis). At that time,
Tolson's poetic reputation rested entirely on *Rendezvous with
America,* published in 1944, which included the much reprinted
"Dark Symphony," awarded first prize four years earlier by
judges Langston Hughes, Arna Bontemps, and Frank Marshall
Davis in a national contest sponsored by the American Negro
Exposition.

Out of abysses of Illiteracy,
Through labyrinths of Lies,
Across waste lands of Disease . . .
We advance!

Out of dead-ends of Poverty,
Through wildernesses of Superstition,
Across barricades of Jim Crowism . . .
We advance!

With the Peoples of the World . . .
We advance!

Like her own *For My People*, Walker wrote, Tolson's poetry reflected "the note of social protest" that had been more popular in the 1930s. But a large part of her article defended Gwendolyn Brooks against charges of obscurantism. Though Walker deplored the return to neoclassical form that characterized postwar poetry, with its emphasis "on technique rather than subject matter" and its turning from social concerns to religious individualism, she said, "Coming after the long complaint of white critics that Negro poets lack form and intellectual acumen, Brooks's careful craftsmanship and sensitive understanding, reflected in *Annie Allen*, are not only personal triumphs but a racial vindication." Tolson, who seems to have read everything, most certainly read Walker's article with its sympathetic reference to his own poetry. At that time, he was beginning his *Libretto for the Republic of Liberia*, which would mark his own turn from direct social protest to a poetry as difficult and obscure as that of any modernist. Walker's defense and justification of Brooks may have spurred and must have supported his own new formal directions.

Discussing a poet's influences is always risky and sometimes profoundly misleading. Tolson, however, was so deliberate in his methods and articulate in discussing his poetic concerns that he helps us to understand the change that he underwent between *Rendezvous* and *Libretto*. As late as 1946, he was still an ardent champion of Carl Sandburg, Edgar Lee Masters, and his friends Langston Hughes and Edwin Markham (author of "The Man with a Hoe"). But he had always experimented with a range of verse forms, from traditional sonnets to stark disyllabics.

> I judge
> My soul
> Eagle
> Nor mole
> A man
> Is what

He saves
From rot.

("Harlem Gallery" and Other Poems, 45)

In addition to the sinewy free verse that characterizes most of "Dark Symphony," *Rendezvous with America* includes sonnets, a variety of meters and rhyme schemes, and many kinds of stanza. Compared to the free verse that comprised *A Gallery of Harlem Portraits, Rendezvous* seemed a return to more traditional forms. But only six years later Tolson wrote about his *Libretto* that "if one wants to be a modern poet, one must study modern poets— and the greatest—Stevens, Rimbaud, Blok, Eliot, Pound et al. I have done this for twenty years. . . . Away with the simple Negro! This is a book to be chewed and digested" (Farnsworth, 167).

> The Parliament of African Peoples signets forever
>   the *Recessional of Europe* and
>   trumpets the abolition of itself:
>   and no nation uses *Felis leo* or
>   *Aquila heliaca* as the emblem of
>   *blut and boden;* and the hyenas
>   whine no more among the bar-
>   ren bones of the seventeen sun-
>   set sultans of Songhai; and the
>   deserts that gave up the ghost
>   to green pastures chant in the
>   ears and teeth of the Dog, in
>   the Rosh Hashana of the Afric
>   calends: *"Honi soit qui mal y pense!"*
>   ("Harlem Gallery" and Other Poems, 187)

What incited this radical shift in poetic strategy by a fifty-year-old poet? What did Tolson hope to accomplish with this belated conversion to what is commonly called high modernism? Because Tolson asked Allen Tate to write the preface for *Libretto* and Karl Shapiro to write the introduction for *Harlem Gallery,*

69

some critics have dealt with his new poetic directions as a gesture to gain the applause of the white critical establishment. Shapiro himself contributed to this viewpoint by attacking Tate as a "confederate of the old school who has no use for Negroes but who will salute an exception to the race. . . . Mr. Tate invites Mr. Tolson to join his country club" (Farnsworth, 171).

It may be more instructive, however, to return to Margaret Walker's essay. Walker, like Tolson a poet of national stature who spent her adult life teaching at an underfunded black southern college, recognized that the "social protest" poetry she had written during the previous decade was by 1950 considered outmoded. The most esteemed white poets were not only emulating T. S. Eliot's return to neoclassic forms, but emulating his orthodox Christianity and reactionary politics. As a poet, Walker worried about the "future of the Negro writing poetry in America," and concluded that that future was bright "only if the future of the world is bright" (112).

Looking at the same situation, Tolson refused to compromise his faith in social progress. He reasoned instead that progress must be made on all fronts, including art. He wrote, "No man escapes his race, his milieu, his class, his moment of history. . . . Great Art does not repeat itself, but, like history, obeys the Heraclitean law of change" (Farnsworth, 213). As a young poet, he had been startled to discover Sandburg's free verse, so unlike the traditional poetry he had studied in school. By 1950 he was, like Walker, convinced that the poetry he had been writing no longer reflected "his moment of history." He had always believed that the distinguishing property of poetry was condensation. Now his reading of his contemporaries convinced him that the historical imperative demanded technical innovations that included extravagant conceits, a surfeit of allusions, complex symbols, and violent cubist juxtaposition. But if he accepted the techniques of high modernism, he had little regard for the reactionary content of its most popular practitioners.

[W]hen you look at my ideas and Eliot's, we're as far apart as hell and heaven. I guess Shapiro, a Jew of the Jews, sees that and takes me under his wing. . . . My work is certainly difficult in metaphors, symbols and juxtaposed ideas. There the similarity between me and Eliot separates. That is only technique, and any artist must use the technique of his time . . . (Farnsworth, 145)

Tolson often teased his students that white people used the library to hide information from them. For years, he had struggled to find an artistic method that would harmonize his own scholarly zeal and his desire for a popular audience. As early as 1943, when he was still composing in the vein of "Dark Symphony" and "Rendezvous with America," he had written with characteristic folksiness in a "Caviar and Cabbage" column,

> Some people say the language of my poetry is very different from the language of "Caviar and Cabbage." Well, when you go to a formal ball of the Big Boys, you have to put on evening clothes. No lie! When I'm at home, among friends, I go about the house in my patched pajamas. A woman doesn't cook cabbage in her Sunday best. In "Caviar and Cabbage" I try to be so simple that only a Howard professor can tell I am a professor. (*Caviar*, 271)

Since at least 1937, and most probably since his student days at Lincoln, Tolson had displayed an appetite for both caviar and cabbage. In an era when the line between high and popular culture was more pronounced, Tolson aspired to speak to a popular audience and to the audience of the ages. This tension holds throughout Tolson's poetry, in all its formal variations. As late as 1964, in *Harlem Gallery*, this tension would be represented in the character of Hideho Heights, "the poet laureate of Lenox Avenue" whose split identity is reflected in

> the bifacial nature of his poetry:
> the racial ballad in the public domain
> and the private poem in the modern vein.
> (*"Harlem Gallery" and Other Poems*, 335)

In the Zulu Club, Hideho recites a ballad about John Henry to wild applause. But when the narrator of the poem takes the drunken poet home one night, he discovers a poem "in the modern idiom" called "E. & O.E." Tolson had published the same poem fifteen years earlier in *Poetry* magazine under his own name. That he reprints the poem as the work of a fictional "People's poet," written in "a sort of Pasternakian secrecy," adds yet another layer of irony to an already difficult poem. Hideho is torn between his identity as a popular entertainer and his realization that "with no poems of Hideho's in World Lit— / he'd be a statistic!"; between his wish to speak to and for his people and his desire to enter the canon of world literature.

> here was the eyesight proof
> that the Color Line, as well as the Party Line,
> splits an artist's identity
> like the vertical which
> Omar's *Is* and *Is-not* cannot define.
>
> (337)

After his discovery of Sandburg, Masters, and the modern idiom, Tolson had composed a Harlem version of *Spoon River Anthology*. With "Rendezvous with America" and "Dark Symphony," Tolson established a poetic reputation in the 1940s as a master of heroic populist rhetoric, a composer of poems that cry out for declamation. (Tolson is reputed to have been a stirring orator, whose recitations moved even those who failed to understand the poems.) But by 1944, Tolson was also gaining a reputation for scholarship. In his review of *Rendezvous with America*, Richard Wright had written perceptively, "Tolson's poetic lines and images sing, affirm, reject, predict, and judge. His vision is informed by the core of Negro experience in America, and his poetry is direct and humanistic. All history, from Genesis to Munich, is his domain" (Flasch, 69).

In 1947, Tolson was appointed poet laureate of the Liberian

Centennial and Peace Exposition. (Duke Ellington was named composer laureate for the same event and composed his "Liberian Suite.") Founded by the American Colonization Society as a refuge for former American slaves, Liberia shared a special bond with Lincoln University, which had been founded as the Ashmun Institute for the purpose of educating Negroes to assume leadership roles in Africa. In his "Caviar and Cabbage" columns, Tolson had criticized the oppression of African inhabitants of Liberia by the descendants of black American colonists. But by the time of Tolson's appointment, William Tubman had been elected president of Liberia on a platform that promised to reconcile these populations in a new national harmony. Tolson now determined to celebrate the dawn of a pan-Africanism that would resolve ethnic strife between Africans, and to praise Liberian independence as harbinger of the liberation from colonial oppression that was soon to sweep the continent . It must be remembered that at the time of Tolson's poem, in 1953, Liberia was the sole independent republic in sub-Saharan Africa. His *Libretto* remains one of the most poignantly optimistic and joyful documents of its era.

> *Liberia?*
> No micro-footnote in a bunioned book
> Homed by a pedant
> With a gelded look:
> You are
> The ladder of survival dawn men saw
> In the quicksilver sparrow that slips
> The eagle's claw!
>
> *Liberia?*
> No side-show barker's bio-accident,
> No corpse of a soul's errand
> To the Dark Continent:
> You are
> The lightning rod of Europe, Canaan's key,

The rope across the abyss,
Mehr licht for the Africa-To-Be!
. . . .
O Calendar of the Century,
red-letter the Republic's birth!
O Hallelujah,
oh, let no *Miserere*
venom the spinal cord of Afric earth!
Selah!
. . . .
O Africa, Mother of Science
. . . *lachen mit vastchekes* . . .
What dread hand,
to make tripartite one august event,
sundered Gondwanaland?
What dread grasp crushed your biceps and
back upon the rack
chaos of chance and change
fouled in Malebolgean isolation?

The poem's epic scope and glorious ebullient juxtapositions are balanced by its extreme compression. Tolson's modernist technical vocabulary relies heavily on far-flung allusions, breathless concision, multilingual internationalism, and hybridized idiom. The *Libretto* closes with a Whitmanic travelogue across a developed Africa. Tolson begins the voyage in the Futurafrique, "the chef d'oeuvre of Liberian Motors," transfers to a "stream-phrased and air-chamoised and sponge-cushioned" train, the *United Nations Limited*, then to the "diesel-engined, fourfold-decked, swan-sleek" ship, the *Bula Matadi*, and finishes the journey on *Le Premier des Noirs* of Pan-African Airways. The poem concludes with a jam-packed list of accomplishments by the Parliament of African Peoples.

As often as the poem was compared to Hart Crane's *The Bridge* for its elevated odic rhetoric, its architecture much more closely resembles Pound's *Cantos*—a pastiche of cross-cultural and multilingual references. But its other distinguishing feature reminds you of Eliot's *The Waste Land*. The twenty-nine-page *Libretto* was followed by sixteen pages of closely spaced notes. For examples:

> 69. *Black pearls.* V. Shakespeare, *Two Gentleman of Verona*, V, i. Also *Othello*, II, i: "Well praised! How if she be black and witty?"
> Mr. J.A. Rogers treats the subject and time and place adequately in *Sex and Race*.
>
> 274. *Lachen mit vastchekes:* "laughing with needles being stuck in you"; ghetto laughter.
>
> 355. *Hearts of rags . . . souls of chalk:* Whitman's epithets for the "floating mass" that vote early and often for bread and circuses. *Hanorish tharah sharinas:* "Man is a being of varied, manifold, and inconstant nature." V. Della Mirandola, *Oration on the Dignity of Man.* Cf. Cunha: "The fantasy of universal suffrage [is] the Hercules' club of our dignity."

Dan McCall wrote that "the *Libretto* is immensely difficult—obscure and referential, composed in several languages and buttressed with now-scholarly, now-sly notes to historiography, anthropology, philosophy, music, odd-lore" (Flasch, 79). Stubbornly, almost perversely, Tolson went to Allen Tate, a conservative Southern Fugitive, for a preface to this difficult poem celebrating the promise of postcolonial Africa! But in 1953, Tate was also among the most powerful of American critics, and it's easy to understand why Tolson thought his support might be crucial. Though the insensitivity of Tate's preface remains embarrassing, he did recognize in the poem "a great gift for language, a profound historical sense, and a first-rate intelligence at work." He compared its dense allusions and elevated diction to Pindar and Hart Crane. Selden Rodman and John Ciardi both picked up Tate's reference to Crane, and in favorable reviews in the *New York Times* and the *Saturday Review of Literature* compared the poem to *The Bridge*. When a selection from the poem appeared in *Poetry* magazine, along with Tate's entire preface, William Carlos Williams noted the event in *Paterson IV* and repeated Tolson's "Selah" to conclude stanzas throughout an entire section of the poem.

> —and to Tolson and to his ode
> and to Liberia and to Allen Tate
> (Give him credit)
> and to the South generally
> *Selah!*
>
> (183)

Langston Hughes and Tolson had been friends and mutual supporters for years. Both were Lincoln alumni. Both had gained reputations for their radical political work during the depression. And as poets, both had begun their careers under the inspiration of Carl Sandburg. Hughes, of course, though younger, had known success much earlier, and had even served as mentor for the older poet. Hughes had been on the panel of judges that awarded Tolson his first literary prize, and frequently included Tolson in the anthologies he assembled. Cosmopolitan, widely read, dazzlingly productive, and dwelling in vibrant Harlem, Hughes was already a literary eminence of international reputation when the graduate student Tolson interviewed him for his thesis. In several "Caviar and Cabbage" columns, Tolson wrote admiringly about Hughes as a grand celebrity whom he was proud to know. And Tolson several times directed college productions of Hughes's plays.

For his part, in 1945, Hughes wrote in the *Chicago Defender*,

> Melvin Tolson is the most famous Negro professor in the Southwest. Students all over that part of the world speak of him, revere him, remember him, and love him. He is a character. He once turned out a debate team that beat Oxford, England. . . . He is a poet of no mean ability, and his book of poems, "Ren-

76

dezvous with America," is a recent fine contribution to American literature. The title poem appeared in that most literate of
literary publications, the ATLANTIC MONTHLY. But Melvin Tolson is no highbrow. Kids from the cottonfields like him. Cow-
punchers understand him. . . . It is not just English he teaches,
but character, and manhood, and womanhood, and love, and
courage, and pride. (Farnsworth, 106)

Hughes was committed to a popular art, both in content and
technique. He wrote with the assurance of a poet who knows his
audience, and with a faith in that audience bred by his early success. As in the *Defender*, he celebrated Tolson as a kind of East
Texas grassroots phenom. Tolson, on the other hand, despite
his epistolary friendships and cherished visits to New York, suffered the anxiety of the poet working in isolation, whose audience is often idealized. As Tolson grew older, he identified
increasingly with Boris Pasternak, writing in a kind of rural
secrecy. While Hughes continued to gain in social and literary
grace, Tolson grew more eccentric and independent. Gradually
Hughes developed reservations about what he perceived as the
increasing pedanticism in Tolson's verse. At one point he
objected to Tolson's rhyme of China and orchestrina: "Nobody
knows what an orchestrina is (that is, nobody of the Race)"
(Rampersad, *II*, 173). Hughes might have been right about most
of the race, and humanity—unless they had attended Wiley and
studied with Professor Tolson. According to his students, the
dictionary was a textbook in every class he taught—and if you
didn't know the meaning of a word, he could always find time to
make you an example of backwoods ignorance.

Hughes and Arna Bontemps had their own reasons to resent
the positive review given Tolson's *Libretto* in the *New York
Times*. Reviewer Selden Rodman had for years neglected to
include Negro poets in the anthologies he edited. So they were
irked when Rodman wrote that the *Libretto* "is not only by all

odds the most considerable poem so far written by an American Negro, but a work of poetic synthesis in the symbolic vein altogether worthy to be discussed in the company of such poems as 'The Waste-Land,' 'The Bridge,' and 'Paterson'" (Farnsworth, 165). Hughes and Bontemps felt that Rodman was using his praise for Tolson to give the back of his hand to every African American poet he had deemed unworthy for his anthologies. In this, Rodman was once again following Tate. In his preface to *Libretto*, Tate had mentioned Hughes and Gwendolyn Brooks by name, admitting that they had written "interesting and even distinguished work," but in a folk idiom that "limited the Negro poet to a provincial mediocrity in which one's feelings about one's difficulties become more important than poetry itself."

Even his admirers frequently criticized Hughes for his facility. Margaret Walker believed that he never revised. And after Hughes's death, Amiri Baraka told an interviewer, "See, what I thought about Langston was that Langston was very glib and facile, that he could write, you know, as easily as breathing, and it's true. What I didn't understand is the consistently high quality of all that he did write" (Rampersad, *II*, 384). But when others attacked Tolson for his obscurantism, an amused Hughes generously defended him. He wrote to Bontemps about *Libretto* that Tolson "told me he was going to write with so many foreign words and footnotes that they would have to pay him some mind!" (Nichols, 320). With the publication of *Harlem Gallery* twelve years later, Hughes again wrote to Bontemps,

> This volume has no footnotes, but a lot of BIG words: (says Tolson)—O Cleobulus / Othales, Solon, Periander, Bias, Chilo, / O Pittacus, / unriddle the phoenix riddle of this? . . . I say, MORE POWER TO YOU, MELVIN B., GO, JACK, GO! That Negro not only reads, but has read! (Nichols, 472).

By 1966, Hughes even included Allen Tate in the "tributary" section of his revised *Poetry of the Negro* anthology, perhaps in recognition of a change in Tate that began with his championing of Tolson.

Advocates for Hughes's popular art have been less sympathetic toward what they see as Tolson's apostasy. In his excellent biography of Hughes, Arnold Rampersad charged that Tolson renounced his earlier "militant pro-Marxism" (Rampersad, *II*, 234) and "gentrified his aesthetic into High Modernism" (193). Don L. Lee (now Haki Madhubuti), reviewing an anthology of black poetry, wrote, "Melvin B. Tolson is represented with some of his less obscure poetry which still exhibits his range and his capacity to lose the people that may read him" (Flasch, 135). The French academic Jean Wagner, author of *Les Poétes Negres des Etats-Unis*, savaged Tolson as "the learned circus-monkey in the Battle Royal of Afro-American literature, with his ridiculous Allen Tate connections" (Rampersad, 390).

Rampersad's and Wagner's comments assume that the new directions in Tolson's poetry signaled an abandoning of his political principles. But Tolson's politics had always been international in theory and local in practice. During the depression, he had put his life on the line organizing sharecroppers. Beginning in 1954, the poet laureate of Liberia was four times elected mayor of the predominantly black town of Langston, Oklahoma. He was still seeking to effect political change, but he also knew the compromises of public office. And unlike Langston Hughes, Tolson did not write to earn his living. He taught a full load of college courses for more than forty years; put in long hours as debate coach, drama teacher, and small-town mayor; and composed poetry after midnight in his basement. In his midforties, Tolson had written in "The Poet":

A Champion of the People versus Kings—
His only martyrdom is poetry:
A hater of the hierarchy of things—

Freedom's need is his necessity.

("Harlem Gallery" and Other Poems, 29)

Tolson didn't change his ideas about championing the people or hating hierarchy. The controversy about his last two books swings instead about ideas of freedom. Does freedom extend to the poet's imagination, or must the poet address the expressed needs of a prescribed community? How does a poet find an audience, and how does an audience find its poet?

Tolson himself wasn't entirely comfortable with the nature of his critical reception, and even joked, "My poetry is of the proletariat, by the proletariat, and for the bourgeoisie" (Nielsen, *Writing Between the Lines,* 54). But Tolson's obsessions in the last two books don't vary far from *Rendezvous with America.* Tolson reinforced attitudes expressed as early as "Caviar and Cabbage" when he read *Black Bourgeoisie,* a work published by Howard University sociologist E. Franklin Frazier in 1957. *Harlem Gallery* is infused with insights drawn from Frazier. In the poem, the black bourgeoisie, represented most vividly in the character of Guy Delaporte III, pose the most oppressive challenge to the African American artist. And the formal experiments of the later poems put Tolson squarely on the side of radicalism and experiment, where he placed Hughes in his thesis. That more expansive form allows him to stretch into regions and voices denied to the oratorical single narrator of his earlier work. Instead of filtering his material through one voice, his poems now contain a multitude of voices that carry his democratic commitment even more effectively. And his legendary sense of humor finds room in his poems smack up against his most earnest declamations. Both contribute to an irony that keeps readers off-balance and demands that you be poised to follow the next line in any direction.

In 1966, Dan McCall, author of a study of Richard Wright, became a colleague of Tolson's at Langston College. During the next year McCall spent a great deal of time with the older man.

At the end of the year, McCall published an article about Tolson in *American Quarterly* in which he paid special attention to the *Libretto*.

> Eliot describes a failure of civilization; the poem establishes a sense of terrible loss. Grace has been withdrawn from the society of Western man. . . . But in reading the *Libretto* one feels a certain "pell-mell joy," resulting from a revolutionary sense of the high comedy of history. . . . Tolson's poetic integrity would not allow him to retreat into the folksiness of Langston Hughes—making things "simple"—nor would it allow him to lose his own voice in mere imitation. He gives us folk-wisdom and out-Pounds Pound to show what is involved in a country which is profoundly both African and American. (Farnsworth, 173)

The following year, when an interviewer asked Tolson about the "out-Pounds Pound" comment, Tolson replied, "Well, I did go to the Africans instead of the Chinese" (Nielsen, *Writing Between the Lines*, 60). Tolson never tired of repeating, and refuting, Gertrude Stein's remark "that the Negro suffers from Nothingness." Mentioned as early as his "Caviar and Cabbage" columns, the comment finds its way into his last poem.

> In the *ostinato*
> of stamping feet and clapping hands,
> the Promethean bard of Lenox Avenue became a
> lost loose-leaf
> as memory vignetted
> Rabelaisian I's of the Boogie-Woogie dynasty
> in barrel houses, at rent parties,
> on riverboats, at wakes:
> The Toothpick, Funky Five, and Tippling Tom!
> Ma Rainey, Countess Willie V., and Aunt Harriet!
> Speckled Red, Skinny Head Pete, and Stormy Weather!
> Listen, Black Boy.
> Did the High Priestess at 27 rue de Fleurus

assert, "The Negro suffers from nothingness!"
Hideho confided like a neophyte on The Walk,
   "Jazz is the marijuana of the Blacks."
In the *tribulum* of dialectics, I juggled the idea:
   then I observed,
"Jazz is the philosophers' egg of the Whites."
      (*"Harlem Gallery" and Other Poems*, 264)

Tolson seemed ever incredulous that Stein, of all people, made such a comment, given that she had propagandized so fiercely for a band of painters inspired by their acquaintance with African sculpture. Was it arrogance or ignorance that dismissed as primitive Africa's fabled and productive civilizations? Tolson's own rich study of Africa is evidenced throughout his work, and the allusions of the *Libretto* are foreshadowed in "The Negro Scholar," written in 1948.

The ground the Negro scholar stands upon
Is fecund with the challenge and tradition

That Ghana knew, and Melle, and Ethiopia,
And Songhai; civilizations black men built
Before the Cambridge wits, the Oxford dons
Gave to the Renaissance a diadem.

Behold the University of Sankore
In Timbuctoo, a summit of the mind!
Behold, behold Black Askia the Great,
The patron-king of scholars, black and white.
      (*Midwest Journal*, 81)

Like the Negro scholar of his poem, in his *Libretto* Tolson stands on fecund historical ground. Through the poem swirl many historical allusions, from the depiction of the Songhai empire, which flourished for the millennium between the seventh and sixteenth centuries, to denunciations of Italy's rape of Ethiopia and South Africa's vicious apartheid. The "Sol" section, which begins with the infamous Middle Passage, becomes a succession of African proverbs that continues for sixteen triplets:

"A stinkbug should not peddle perfume.
The tide that ebbs will flow again.
A louse that bites is in

"the inner shirt. An open door
sees both inside and out. The saw
that severs the topmost limb

"comes from the ground. God saves the black
man's soul but not his buttocks from
the white man's lash. The mouse

"as artist paints a mouse that chases
a cat. The diplomat's lie is fat
at home and lean abroad.

Melvin Tolson traveled beyond U.S. borders only once in his life, at the invitation of the Liberian government to attend President Tubman's third inauguration in Monrovia in 1955. On the way home, he stopped in Paris for a week, where Melvin Jr. was studying at the Sorbonne and where the Tolsons spent an afternoon with Richard Wright. Like William Carlos Williams, at fifty-five Tolson still had to underwrite the publication of his poems. Unlike Williams, the expense of publication challenged Tolson's means. He was able to pay Twayne $650 to publish *Libretto* and still find $100 to send to his son Wiley as a wedding gift, but having spent that $750 he could not afford to travel to the wedding (Farnsworth, 201).

After an itinerant Missouri childhood following his preacher father from small church to small church, Tolson spent his entire adult life at small Negro colleges in East Texas and Oklahoma. He glimpsed the possibilities of Harlem during his year of graduate study at the beginning of the depression, and subsequent treasured trips to New York, where he sometimes stayed with his friend, V. F. Calverton. In the last years of his life, he frequently visited family in Detroit, and often traveled to New York City on literary business. But his internationalist vision was nurtured primarily by books, and his poems are celebrations of a literary, even pedantic, liberation. While Williams was searching for a modern American idiom, Tolson was seeking a modern international idiom—through which the Afro-American subject would at last stride boldly onto the stage of world literature. While the first book of *Harlem Gallery* reconciled and integrated many of the concerns voiced abruptly and fragmentally in *Libretto*, and in many ways is more satisfying, it was the *Libretto* that successfully thrust Tolson onto that world stage—or maybe we should say world library. A stage implies an audience of some magnitude. I prefer to think of the professor proclaiming a new dawn as he writes after midnight in the basement workshop of his small house in Langston, Oklahoma—a basement where he also entertained guests and which he called the Zulu Club.

Opening the Field
The New American Poetry

*B*y the time that Melvin B. Tolson was composing *Libretto for the Republic of Liberia,* a group of younger poets had already dismissed the formalism of Eliot and his New Critic followers as old hat. Their "new" position was much closer to that of Langston Hughes and others whom Tolson perceived as outmoded, that is, having yet to learn—or advance—the lessons of Eliotic modernism. Inspired by action painting and bebop, these younger poets valued spontaneity, movement, and authentic expression. Though New Critics ruled the established magazines and publishing houses, this new audience was looking for something different, something having as much to do with freedom as form, and finding it in obscure magazines and readings in bars and coffeehouses. In 1960, many of these poets were published by a commercial press for the first time when their poems were gathered in *The New American Poetry, 1946–1960.* Editor Donald Allen claimed for its contributors "one common characteristic: total rejection of all those qualities typical of academic verse."

The extravagance of that "total" characterizes the hyperbolic gestures of that dawn of the atomic age. But what precisely were these poets rejecting? Referring to Elgar's "Enigma" Variations,

Virgil Thomson wrote, "I call them academic because I think the composer's interest in the musical devices he was employing was greater than his effort toward a direct and forceful expression of anything in particular" (Thomson, 189). By 1950, the New Critical focus on poetic devices must have struck young poets as at least indifferent to content. Direct and forceful expression was certainly discouraged, and often disparaged. According to Robert Creeley,

> In the forties, when I was in college, it was considered literally bad taste to have an active interest in [Whitman's] writing. . . . There was a persistent embarrassment that this naively affirmative poet might affect one's own somewhat cynical wisdoms. Too, in so far as this was a time of intensively didactic criticism, what was one to do with Whitman, even if one read him? He went on and on, he seemed to lack "structure," he yielded to no "critical apparatus" then to hand. (Creeley, 3–4)

Kenneth Koch put it more hilariously in "Fresh Air," a poem that in its attack on "the poetry / Written by the men with their eyes on the myth / And the Missus and the midterms," may well have served as *The New American Poetry*'s manifesto.

> Who are the great poets of our time and what are their names?
> Yeats of the baleful influence, Auden of the baleful influence,
>   Eliot of the baleful influence . . .
> Where are young poets in America, they are trembling in
>   publishing houses and universities,
> Above all they are trembling in universities, they are bathing
>   the library steps with their spit,
> They are gargling out innocuous (to whom?) poems about
>   maple trees and their children,
> Sometimes they brave a subject like the Villa d'Este or a
>   lighthouse in Rhode Island,
> Oh what worms they are! they wish to perfect their form.
> (Allen, 231)

Now it demands an act of imagination to appreciate the rebellious character of *The New American Poetry*, since by comparison to decades such as the 1930s or 1970s its cast seems narrow. Among its forty-four contributors LeRoi Jones was the only African American. Nor did editor Donald Allen mention in his list of predecessors to this poetry one African American poet—not Langston Hughes nor Melvin Tolson, Margaret Walker, or Gwendolyn Brooks. His introduction did acknowledge H.D., Marianne Moore, and Elizabeth Bishop. But he included only four women in the anthology: Helen Adam, Madeline Gleason, Barbara Guest, and Denise Levertov.

As incredible as these numbers are, they probably overstate the anthology's diversity. On closer inspection, the group seems even more homogeneous in its attitudes. Legal segregation and the civil rights movement that opposed it are seldom mentioned; the preferred word for African Americans is *nigger*. A fear of and hostility toward women surfaces again and again. As Grace Paley has said more generally about Beat writing, "I thought they were nice, nice to see all those boys, and nice to see all those sexual feelings, but I knew it wasn't written for me at all" (Bach and Hall, 90).

But in 1960 American culture conformed to such a narrow standard that Donald Allen's anthology created quite a stir—and reaction. Writing in the *New Yorker*, Louise Bogan asked, "Does this new poetry arise from sources largely amateur, exhibitionistic, or otherwise out of hand? . . . [D]oes their violence stem from a deliberate attempt to extend consciousness, or are many of them actually out of control?" (200). Lorenzo Thomas, seventeen when the anthology was published, saw it from the other side of the generation gap.

[P]erhaps the academic institution that called itself "American poetry" in the 1950s *was* just that much of a Potemkin village that the appearance of genuine villagers exposed its much-chewed scenery for everyone. . . . *The New American Poetry* was a perfect introduction to the cultural confrontations of the 1960s. Just as that decade has permanently destabilized the uniformity of costume in everyday life (and it's not merely a matter of hat and gloves being superseded by a new standard of blue jeans and tennis), the Allen anthology disrupted the poetic fashion of the 1950s—which was marked by a conformity that reflected the gray happiness of Ike's America. *The New American Poetry* made a new set of approaches to writing poetry accessible.

A more dangerous interpretation might be that the poetic seismograph was really recording the shattering of certain 19th Century fictions of a homogeneous WASP culture. (Thomas, 153)

The anthology was countered by one edited by Donald Hall, Robert Pack, and Louis Simpson that collected the poets of the academies and conservative publications. The War of the Poetry Anthologies was on. On one side were the beatniks, boys who celebrated "all those sexual feelings," many of whom were pacifists and anarchists, all opposed to New Critical hegemony. On the other were the young admirers of Eliot, Tate, Ransom, and Frost, whose response to the war years was to embrace a return to a social hierarchy most eloquently expressed in iambic pentameter.

Looking back from the Reagan era, Donald Hall attempted to downplay the fierce partisanship of the "war of the poetry anthologies" to which he contributed as much as anyone. As poetry editor of the *Paris Review* in the 1950s, Hall regularly published James Dickey, W. D. Snodgrass, Geoffrey Hill, Adrienne Rich, James Wright, Robert Bly, Thom Gunn, and Simpson. Though ten years later most of these poets were themselves writing in "open poetry," in 1960 they were known for their devotion to traditional forms. Hall rejected submissions from Frank O'Hara and Allen Ginsberg, and in a published article insulted Robert Creeley. Yet, Hall insists, by 1965 that war was over.

As the 1960s unfolded and the society was wracked by the turmoil of civil rights agitation, Vietnam War protests, riots and arson, dropouts and turn-ons, widespread police and military harassment culminating in the murder of students on state college campuses at Jackson, Mississippi, and Kent, Ohio—the poetry "wars" came to seem small potatoes. Before the more violent assault on American society, aesthetic differences paled in import. An uneasy truce was effected among poets who, whatever form they chose to write in, marched in the streets side by side.

Hall has said that he was "abashed by the rigidity that defended [his] citadel" and tired of being "Archbishop of Academic Poetry" (*Death to the Death*, 46). He fondly recalls that he, Creeley, Bly, and Gary Snyder sang "Yellow Submarine" in the aisle of a plane en route to an antiwar reading. When he came to edit another anthology for Penguin, he included the aisle-warblers and Denise Levertov—though still excluding Ginsberg and O'Hara. He recommended his former student Tom Clark to succeed him as poetry editor at *Paris Review*, and invited Ted Berrigan to be his houseguest at Ann Arbor, even though Berrigan stole all his pills. (Clark and Berrigan were closely associated with many of the "New American poets.")

Indeed, Hall reminds us again and again that the anthology war was largely a competition among classmates. John Ashbery, L. E. Sissman, Kenneth Koch, Peter Davison, Frank O'Hara, Robert Bly, Robert Creeley, Kenward Elmslie, and even Adrienne Rich (Radcliffe) were at Harvard during the same years as Hall. So was Mitchell Goodman, a poet and novelist who married Denise Levertov. Their writing instructors included John Ciardi and Archibald MacLeish. Richard Wilbur was around campus as a fellow; Richard Eberhart, Robert Frost, and Robert Lowell were living in Cambridge. Hall admits that the lot were ambitious and the competition murderous, but claims that the principal division was between those inspired by Yeats and Hardy (Hall's crew) and those taken with Wallace Stevens and Auden (Ashbery, O'Hara, Koch, Elmslie).

This gives a different slant to the war of the anthologies, with some of the animus between the factions stemming back to undergraduate competition and slights actual and perceived. Poetic politics gets reduced to personal relations. Inclusion or exclusion from an anthology depends more on remarks made at undergraduate bashes than on the quality of a particular poem. The gap between antagonists, though perhaps more deep-set and to the bone, loses aesthetic and political significance.

Hall's forthright witness would persuade us that ambition is intrinsic to poetry, that every poet wishes to measure up against the greats, just as young ballplayers dream of being compared to Barry Bonds or Pedro Martinez. But the Legends of Poetry don't compete on the same field nor to the same ends. The language of poetry evolves with the languages of humans, is modified by circumstance and value, is composed for a panoply of occasions. Even those who attend Harvard bring idiosyncratic luggage, learn conflicting lessons, carry off conflicting ambitions. And then there are so many others.

> who passed through universities with radiant cool eyes
>> hallucinating Arkansas and Blake-light tragedy among the
>> scholars of war,
> who were expelled from the academies for crazy & publishing
>> obscene odes on the windows of the skull,
> who cowered in unshaven rooms in underwear, burning their
>> money in wastebaskets and listening to the Terror through
>> the wall . . .
> who lit cigarettes in boxcars boxcars boxcars racketing through
>> snow toward lonesome farms in grandfather night,
> who studied Plotinus Poe St. John of the Cross telepathy and

bop kaballa because the cosmos instinctively vibrated at
    their feet in Kansas,
who loned it through the streets of Idaho seeking visionary
    indian angels who were visionary indian angels . . .
                 (Ginsberg, from *Howl*, in Allen, 182–84)

Mercury! Poet of Heaven, you old thief, deliver me
from this ravel-streeted, louse-ridden, down-river,
gutter-sniping, rent-gouging, hard-hearted,
                  complacent provincial town,
where they have forgotten all that made this country the
belly of courage, the body of beauty, the hands of heresy,
the legs of the individual spirit, the heart of song!
                 (Blackburn, from "Sirventes,"
                        in Allen, 74)

Ptarmigan hunt for bugs in the snow
Bear peers through the wall at noon
Deer crowd up to see the lamp
A mouse nearly drowns in the honey
I see my bootprints mingle with deer-foot
Bear-paw mule-shoe in the dusty path to the privy
        (Whalen, from "Sourdough Mountain Lookout,"
                      in Allen, 284)

No, I doubt I'd be that kind of father
not rural not snow no quiet window
but hot smelly tight New York City
seven flights up, roaches and rats in the walls
a fat Reichian wife screeching over potatoes, Get a job!
And five nose-running brats in love with Batman
             (Corso, from "Marriage," in Allen, 211)

Morning again, nothing has to be done
         maybe buy a piano or make fudge
At least clean the room up, for sure like my farther
  I've done flick the ashes & buts over the bedside on the floor.

But frist of all wipe my glasses and drink the water
         to clean the smelly mouth.
A nock on the door, a cat walks in, behind her the Zoo's baby
    elephant demanding pancaks—I can't stand hallucinations
    any more.
                (Orlovsky, from "Second Poem," in Allen, 213)

Were poets such as Gregory Corso, Peter Orlovsky, or Ray
Bremser working-class poets? Well, not exactly. Though from
humble origins, they saw themselves not as workers but as
refuseniks, dropouts, drug addicts—outsiders who had been
involuntarily confined, in prisons, reform schools, mental hospi-
tals, or some combination of the three. They didn't want a
square job and didn't envy those who did; those who "sold out"
for middle-class conveniences earned their opprobrium. I recall
recommending Kerouac and Ginsberg to a friend forming a literacy class for working-class Vermonters, only to be rebuffed by
the reply, "But they're Columbia boys!" But at the height of the
Cold War, for many young people they represented the only
rebellion around against conformist American values.

During the 1960s, these "outsider" voices in *The New American
Poetry* inspired me and many of my friends too young to recall the
"proletarian poets" of the 1930s or to know more esoteric alternatives from the 1950s. It wasn't necessary that their poems be
among our favorites in the anthology, simply that they be included
among the other poets, signaling to our imaginations a wilder possibility. Phil Whalen, Gary Snyder, Lew Welch, Paul Blackburn—
we searched out everything they had written, astounded that people who had jobs like washing lab equipment or driving a taxi were
respected as poets. In a 1992 interview with the *Paris Review*, Gary
Snyder explained some of the differences between the "New
Poetry" and the mainstream poetry that it challenged.

    I: What were you finding in Chinese poetry at that time?
    GS: The secular quality, the engagement with history, the

avoidance of theology or of elaborate symbolism or metaphor, the spirit of friendship, the openness to work, and, of course, the sensibility for nature. For me it was a very useful balancing force to set beside Sidney, *The Faerie Queene*, Renaissance literature, Dante. The occidental tradition is symbolic, theological, and mythological, and the Chinese is paradoxically more, shall we say, modern, in that it is secular in its focus on history or nature. That gave me a push. (Plimpton, 279)

Snyder's college roommate and friend Philip Whalen began a 1999 interview with David Meltzer by listing the jobs he had held since graduating from college, beginning with a year in an airplane factory and including working for the Forest Service as a lookout, "washing laboratory glassware" at the Poultry Husbandry Department at Berkeley, working for a friend who was a judge in Oregon, and teaching English for thirteen years in Kyoto, Japan. He didn't separate the ways he earned his living from his friendships, writing, or longtime Zen practice, but offered all as pertinent to the subject, Philip Whalen. Just as a lawyer friend of mine was initially drawn to Wallace Stevens by the example of a poet who managed a successful legal career, I remember the excitement with which I first encountered Snyder and Whalen, poets who worked for a living at the same kinds of jobs I had held myself. Perhaps I too could attend poetry readings and submit poems to magazines, even though I hadn't been to Harvard, lacked a résumé of grants and fellowships, or paid my rent by loading trucks, unloading boats, or working in kitchens.

But even among contributors to the anthology, there were class-based tensions. Paul Blackburn was a hero of the Lower East Side poetry scene and founder of several reading series. When his *Collected Poems* were published, Marjorie Perloff's sardonic review set him up against the genius of Frank O'Hara so she could dismiss him as "second string." (For good measure, she took the opportunity to insult poets Joe Ceravolo and Dick

Gallup, two contributors to the *Anthology of New York Poets* notable for not belonging to "some elegant minority." Ceravolo worked as an hydraulic engineer in northern New Jersey; Gallup has been a San Francisco taxi driver for many years. Though Perloff is one of our most distinguished academic critics, every imagination has its limits.)

At a panel discussion of Blackburn that I later attended at the Poetry Project, I was not surprised to hear the panelists respond to Perloff's attack, but was startled by the approach. Edith Jarolim, editor of Blackburn's *Collected Poems*, understandably attacked Perloff's review as class-based. Blackburn, Jarolim told the sympathetic downtown crowd, was "our poet," singer of the sidewalks and subways. Of course, Jarolim explained, Perloff would be attracted to the poets of the elegant minority, such as O'Hara and John Cage. When I mentioned Jarolim's response to Ron and Pat Padgett, Ron said, "When you mentioned Blackburn, I immediately thought 'downtown poet.'" But Pat defended O'Hara as being from "kind of a working-class background himself." And they felt it unfair to compare almost any poet to O'Hara.

As a college student, two of the books I cherished most were Blackburn's *The Cities* and O'Hara's *Lunch Poems*. Since then, I have grown only more appreciative of O'Hara's inimitable poetry. Blackburn's legendary generosity fostered a horde of imitators, whose widely published work sometimes obscures the freshness of Blackburn's own poems. Saddened by his premature death, his friends published much work that the poet might have suppressed or further refined. Blackburn's work is also marred by attitudes toward women too prevalent during his lifetime. But there are still poems and stretches in Blackburn that are as melodious and moving as any written by his contemporaries—which, because of his keen ear for the idioms of street speech, may appeal with special force to those who do not belong to an elegant minority. While I wouldn't dispute Perloff's claims for

O'Hara, her attack on Blackburn rankled me as at least insensitive to issues of class.

Yet Blackburn's poems, for their downtown character, can
not be called poems of the working class, in the way that the proletarian poets of the 1930s claimed to be representative. In the
aftermath of World War II, class distinctions in the United
States were felt as strongly as ever, but people were losing the
vocabulary to frame them. Perhaps it was advertising, perhaps
just television, but in the "Great Society" truck drivers, cops,
secretaries, carpenters, clerks, and plumbers began to describe
themselves as "middle class." As they yielded their working-class
identity, their children replaced it with longings and lacks: longing for managerial-class perks and portfolios, a new car, or college degree. The only classes left were More and Less, Haves
and Have-Nots, Squares and Beatniks, the Organization Man
and the Outsider, the Rich and the Not Rich. As Denise Levertov wrote in a letter to William Carlos Williams: "All the passion
and illusion of the thirties that fizzled out with the war is denied
to one in the '50's because one's damned if one's going to be
tricked and bamboozled" (MacGowan, 57).

Despite its insensitivity to problems of race and gender, *The
New American Poetry* signaled an opening of the field to prospec-
tive poets of diverse social backgrounds. Like the Declaration of
Independence, it offered freedom to those who were not represented in its drafting. Other things were obviously happening in
the country, and it's out of line to claim for the anthology any
credit for the burgeoning black arts movement of the late 1960s
or the rise of feminism. Lorenzo Thomas's *Extraordinary Measures* and Aldon Nielsen's *Black Chant* provide invaluable testi-
mony about African American avant-garde poets of the era
whose work was sadly excluded from almost all the "white"
anthologies, including those of the New American crowd. In
addition to the four women in the anthology, Gwendolyn
Brooks, Muriel Rukeyser, Diane di Prima, and others gave

example to young women poets. But by foregrounding content and connecting poetic measure to the individual breath, the anthology expanded the boundaries of American poetry and signaled a welter of different voices.

If only five poets in the anthology were African American or women, a large number of them were homosexuals at a time when homosexuals were viciously scorned and oppressed. During a decade dominated by World War II vets, a number of these poets were pacifists, conscientious objectors, or recipients of dishonorable discharges. Although the poets from the East Coast still looked to Europe, a number of West Coast poets looked to Asia. Many were or later became Buddhists. All were seeking an alternative to the status quo of Eisenhower America, an opening or enlargement of poetic space.

Only twelve years old when the anthology was published, by the time I got to college I had made my choice. I admired many poets that we studied in class, including T. S. Eliot, Robert Lowell, Robert Frost, and W. H. Auden. (We got lots of Eliot; Pound, still confined in St. Elizabeth's, was not read. At the University of Wisconsin in 1970, a progressive young professor still thought it daring to add Williams to his syllabus.) But *The New American Poetry* was another world, one we visited on our own time and talked about over beer, coffee, and dope. Every poem was an antidote to the authoritarianism of Eliot and the New Critical tradition. Even when the poets were Christians, such as Brother Antoninus or Jack Kerouac, they revived the benign tradition of St. Francis in "A Canticle to the Waterbirds" or composed Buddhist blues. And if few of the poets were working class, at least Whalen, Snyder, Ginsberg, Blackburn, Kerouac, and Lew Welch showed familiarity with manual work, respect for those who did it, and comfort with working-class speech and milieus. There was a healthy Whitmanic respect for occupations, and popping up throughout, the dream of a classless society.

the beauty of America, neither cool jazz nor devoured Egyptian
    heroes, lies in
lives in the darkness I inhabit in the midst of sterile millions

the only truth is face to face, the poem whose words become
    your mouth
and dying in black and white we fight for what we love, not are
                  (O'Hara, "Ode: Salute to the
              French Netro Poets," in Allen, 254)

Literary Men in Blue Jeans
Ted Berrigan and
Ron Padgett

Since its publication in 1960 *The New American Poetry* has continued to be the landmark American poetry anthology of the second half of the twentieth century. The cover of the recent reprint issued by the University of California Press proclaims "more than 100,000 copies sold." Though that's a meager figure for books other than poetry and computes to less than three thousand copies a year, it's an impressive figure for a poetry anthology. In addition, books by contributors Allen Ginsberg, Jack Kerouac, Lawrence Ferlinghetti, Gregory Corso, and Gary Snyder have also sold well and remain in print fifty years after their first edition. Paul Hoover built on this foundation his expansive *Postmodern American Poetry*, and *The New American Poetry* figures more prominently in the afterword Ron Silliman wrote for his revised *In the American Tree* (1999) than it did in his preface to the original 1986 edition. Though editors Donald Allen and George Butterick substantially revised *The New American Poetry* in 1982 and retitled it *The Postmoderns*, it is the original collection that remains in print. What is the call of this outdated anthology of mostly white male poets that continues to attract readers in a world that has changed drastically? Perhaps it is the vision of an alternative America, liberated from fundamentalist repression and cash value morality, that led and leads readers, particularly young readers, to these poets. Their pulsing lines continue to be admired by aspiring poets, but I suspect it's the strains of intellectual and sensual liberation, anarchism, pacifism, Zen Buddhism, sensitivity to nonhuman nature, and general rebellion and restlessness that attract other readers.

At the same time that *The New American Poetry* gathered readers, the civil rights struggle fostered the black arts movement and gained national recognition for Amiri Baraka, David Henderson, Sonia Sanchez, Jayne Cortez, Larry Neal, Carolyn Rodgers, Nikki Giovanni, Ishmael Reed, Quincy Troupe, and Haki Madhubuti. With the revival of the feminist movement, women were rediscovering predecessors such as Zora Neale Hurston, Meridel LeSueur, and Tillie Olsen. Alice Walker, Anne Waldman, Bernadette Mayer, June Jordan, Diane di Prima, Hettie Jones, Diane Wakoski, Grace Paley, Rochelle Owens, and Adrienne Rich published before 1970. Maureen Owen, Susan and Fanny Howe, Lucille Clifton, Sharon Olds, Alice Notley, Cleopatra Mathis, Patricia Spears Jones, and Alicia Ostriker began publishing in the next decade. After Stonewall, the burgeoning gay and lesbian movements encouraged a new openness among poets such as Tim Dlugos, Eileen Myles, Dennis Cooper, Steven Hall, Judy Grahn, and Olga Broumas.

Throughout this burgeoning of populist poets, class lines were being obscured. Well, not entirely. The Academy of American Poets remained a high-rent club for comfortable white men. When asked why Gwendolyn Brooks was not a member of the academy's Board of Chancellors, James Merrill reportedly replied, "I just don't think she's a Master." Was this boorish insensitivity to connotation, or simply the mot juste for admittance to the last bastion of antebellum gentility?

There were low-rent alternatives, most of them downtown. Perhaps the most notable were the Poetry Project at St. Mark's

Church In-the-Bowery and, later, the Nuyorican Café. Not only could you feel comfortable attending a reading at the church in jeans and T-shirt, casual dress was so common that even the elegant John Ashbery dressed down to flannel shirt and jeans to read there. At Project benefits, penniless poets sat among rock stars, actors, and rich patrons. The Nuyorican Café at that time occupied a small storefront on East Sixth Street. Inside were a bar, a stage, and maybe twenty chairs. Most evenings the same few regulars took turns reciting their poems to each other, while patrons drifted in and out, but because Miguel Piñero, Lucky Cienfuegos, and Miguel Algarin were heavily involved with Joe Papp's Public Theater, celebrities of stage and screen also frequently showed up. It was a community anyone could enter without class credentials. Most of both audiences lived in neighborhood tenements that had yet to be gentrified. Though my friends and I lived in a building where we had no heat or hot water during the first two winters I lived there, we felt ourselves doubly lucky. Not only was rent cheap, but many of the other tenants were poets, including Allen Ginsberg. It wasn't rare to take out your trash and run into Andrei Voznezhensky or Robert Creeley.

In 1969 I graduated from Siena College, a small Roman Catholic commuter college in Loudonville, New York. The first college graduate in my extended family, I sailed through school with so many scholarships that I made money by attending college. I continued to work with my stepfather on his moving van, maintained a daily newspaper delivery route to newsstands and slot boxes, and earned enough money bowling on TV to buy my parents a small swimming pool that enveloped the tiny backyard of their tract house. At the urging of several of my teachers, I decided to enter the graduate program in English literature at the University of Wisconsin in Madison. My parents thought it odd that a twenty-one-year-old man would wish to continue in school, but I always paid my own way, received aid from Wisconsin, and might be deferred from serving in Vietnam for another couple years, so they didn't object.

During my years at Siena I made friends with several other "brown-baggers" (commuter students) with literary interests. When we were not in class or the library or the gym, we spent our time at a table in the commuter cafeteria, known as "the pit," discussing literature, politics, and philosophy. We were all from blue-collar backgrounds, and the only literary people we had ever known were professors and priests. In 1969 none of us was entering the priesthood, but several of us were heading to state universities to prolong our literary apprenticeships. Most impressive was the clarity of my pal Jim Legasse, who was off to Ohio State, where, he had already determined, he was going to write a doctoral thesis on James Thomson, author of *The Seasons.* I had collected more than forty credits in undergrad lit courses, but with total disregard to period or concentration. Mostly I just signed up for what struck my fancy—or was offered that term. I did respond strongly to the poems of Ben Jonson and John Donne, so went to Madison with some vague idea about the seventeenth century.

The poets with whom I spent most of my time at Madison were Wordsworth and Andrew Marvell. But I also derived a contemporary reading list from *The New American Poetry.* By the mid-1960s, copies of Allen Ginsberg's *Howl* and Ferlinghetti's *Coney Island of the Mind* were everywhere. It was easy to find books by Olson, Creeley, Levertov, Corso, and Duncan. But in Madison bookstores you could also find O'Hara's *Lunch Poems* and *Meditations in an Emergency,* Paul Blackburn's *The Cities,* Kenneth Koch's *Thank You,* Gary Snyder's *Riprap* and *The Back Country,* LeRoi Jones's *The Dead Lecturer,* and even first editions of John Wieners's *Hotel Wentley Poems.* Most fortunate for me, in the university library I also came across Ted Berrigan's *Many Happy Returns* and Ron Padgett's *Great Balls of Fire.* Here was the next generation of poets, and even more than the poets in the anthology, they were the first poets who seemed to be writing in my language.

I didn't consider Berrigan and Padgett to be as imposing as Frank O'Hara or Charles Olson, because they weren't as quick as O'Hara or as authoritative as Olson. And if I had learned anything about poetry, it was that it was supposed to be condensed and difficult. But more than any poets I had ever read, Berrigan and Padgett seemed to be recognizable people living in a familiar world—with incredible zest and resourceful imagination. These guys were making poems out of materials that lay to hand, and they were doing so without the heavy existential angst that afflicted so many of the New American poets. Instead they were fresh, totally irreverent smart-asses grabbing words that sailed so near in the air that it was almost impossible to make them stay on the page. They were not archaeologists of morning, not visionary bards, not wailing in the wilderness, not even Harvard wits. They were neither desperate nor frail nor mystic initiates. They were simply young American poets of talent but no special privilege.

The poets that I met from the generation preceding them were often bearing existential burdens that precluded common pleasures. I always think of Gregory Corso's putdown of Joel Oppenheimer, "Oh, you're one of those domestic poets." You rarely think of marriage and the Beats; though few served in the military, they shared the barracks chauvinism of the World War II generation. Few were comfortable for any length of time in the company of women. Berrigan and Padgett weren't yet feminists, but they were "domestic poets" who enjoyed and wrote about family life. They didn't hold themselves apart or above their neighbors, didn't come on like illuminati or initiates. Their sense of humor was often crude and impersonal; they said things that you might hear in a dugout or locker room. I didn't feel as if I had to rid myself of my past before I could be born into poetry; I could carry everything along, so long as I continued to write like crazy. Because of their reading of the New York poets as well as the Beats, they were children of Stein *and* Whitman. That is, they recognized the genius of Stein's demotic experiments and the democratic embrace of Whitman, without vaunting an avant-garde self-importance. They made you feel that the distinction between major and minor poetry was for academics; they pissed on hierarchy in any form. Their spirit was anarchic, fun-loving, amiable, irreverent, tolerant, and peaceable. Their books fanned my desire to go to New York and have a good time writing poems and meeting other poets and artists.

The first reading I attended in New York was at the Gotham Book Mart. Ron Padgett, Maureen Owen, and Larry Fagin were the readers; perhaps they had all recently published books. I knew no one in attendance and hugged closely to the upstairs gallery walls, enduring the interminable party chat between the announced and actual time of reading. Once it began, I was challenged and delighted, and knew I had at last, at the ancient age of twenty-five, come to the right spot. I rued only that it had taken me so long to find this place.

After that evening, I began to regularly attend poetry readings in New York City—at Dr. Generosity's, the Tin Palace, the Donnell Library, the Ear Inn, occasionally the Ninety-second Street Y, Chumley's, the New School for Social Research, the Cedar Tavern, the West End, the White Horse, and numerous other bars, bookstores, art galleries, and lofts where readings were held for an evening, a season, or several years. At many of these I was a regular on weekend afternoons or midweek evenings, but once Michael Scholnick and I became roommates in our sixth floor walk-up on east Ninth Street, we began to spend four or five nights a week at the St. Mark's Poetry Project or Nuyorican Café. Many nights we would hit both, beginning the evening with a reading at St. Mark's Church, then meandering to Sixth Street afterward, where the old Nuyorican Café remained ablaze with voices until early in the morning. For two years I made a living by driving cab, and though I usually drove five or six nights a week, the schedule was flexible. I didn't have to decide whether I was working that night until it came time for shape-up. I quit only after being hired as a recording engineer for the Talking Books division of the Foundation for the Blind— a plum of a job where I was actually paid to listen to Broadway's best read everything from Gothic romances and shoot-'em-ups to *The Sound and the Fury* and the poems of Edna St. Vincent Millay. Because most of the actors were performing uptown in the evening, we didn't begin recording until 10:00 A.M., allowing me time after the Poetry Project or the Nuyorican to write into the early mornings.

By the time I arrived in New York, it was no longer novel for children of the working class to pursue careers as poets or painters. The democratization of the art world was tied closely to the explosion of higher education in this country. Those who reached college age in the United States between 1945 and 1980 had unprecedented access to postsecondary education. In most states, tuition at state universities for in-state residents was nominal or free. Still, as we moved through the New York art world, we remained uncomfortable about our origins. The size of the chips on our shoulders made it almost impossible to fit through some of the doors that were opened for us. Few from the working class understood that success as an artist was achieved with the same social skills that made any professional successful—and those who did know it didn't necessarily have those skills.

Berrigan and Padgett had been fortunate to bring with them to New York their cohort from Tulsa, Oklahoma. They met when Padgett was a high school student working in a bookstore, Berrigan a Korean War vet studying on the GI bill at Tulsa University. Pat Padgett, the poet Dick Gallup, and writer and artist

Joe Brainard were from Tulsa too. Though Ron Padgett later described Gallup's and Brainard's fathers as "lunch-pail kind of guys" and his own family as "lower class," the young Tulsans tended to view themselves as bohemian poets and artists, a group that less literary Tulsans often lumped with "beatniks" and even "Commies." *The Outsider*, by Colin Wilson, had been a "big book" for the entire group.

For Padgett, his attendance and graduation from Columbia College (the Ivy one) complicated his sense of class. He saw immediately that the name of his alma mater gained him a certain entry into polite conversation. People responded to him differently than if he identified himself as the son of a bootlegger. And by being a poet in 1960s New York, he gained another *passe partout*. During an interview I conducted with Ron and Pat Padgett, Ron said, "The one thing I really liked about being a poet in New York is that it gave one a lot of social mobility. Not that one moved up or down in one's station. It's almost as if one weren't in a station in New York. So one night I would find myself walking the streets of the lower east side with Harry Fainlight, the next night I'd be at a salon or party at Lita Hornick's, or I would be at Andy Warhol's, or at a party at the Tibor de Nagy gallery and I'd meet Larry Rivers. . . . I could be in all kinds of milieus, from real uptown to real downtown. I felt that was terrific. That was exactly the kind of nondefinition of my status that I was looking for, that I wanted to perpetuate."

When I asked him, "After attending Columbia, living in France, about forty years of being a poet in New York, do you think that your writing is still inflected in any way by your lower-class background?"

Ron: Yes. (Silence.) You asked me a yes-or-no question. The answer is yes.

I: How?

Ron: Oh no, I knew you were going to say that. It's hard for me to distinguish the influence of class in my work. It's as if a plate of food's in front of you with different things like potatoes and peas on it. Say the peas are your class. While you're eating them it's very clear what they are. But once you're finished dinner, it's not so clear anymore what's happening to them. I think that early influences, whether artistic or any kind, become so transformed throughout one's life that it's not that they're not there anymore, it's just that they take subtle and different shapes, blended to such a degree with the other things you are that it's very hard to sort them out. However, I could go through some of my poems and point out ways in which the class I grew up in has affected what the work tries to talk about and doesn't try to talk about, the level of diction, the tendency to avoid large claims or make definitive statements, a penchant for the colloquial. I can't seem to get away from those tendencies. I'm not sure that I want to, although it would be interesting to try to write a *Paradise Lost* with elevated diction and enormous claims. I've thought about ways that I might do that, but I can't figure out *a* way to do it.

Pat: Do you think that the fact that you don't want to make any large claim is a result of coming from the working class?

Ron: Partly. Because there's a fear of pretension among a lot of the working-class people I know. Putting on airs is very inappropriate: You're stepping out of your class, you're pretending you're something you're not, you're trying to be highfalutin'. Along with that fear comes a modesty that says, No, you can't do that. You can't say, "Of arms and the man I sing."

Pat: It's not just a matter of diction then.

Ron: No. It's also that large claims imply a presumption of authority. Lower-class people think that they don't have any authority. Maybe subconsciously they feel that they *shouldn't* have any authority.

Pat: They don't have the wherewithal.

Ron: If they did, why are they near the bottom of the social ladder? I have rarely worried about where I am on the social ladder, but it *is* hard for me to get up on a soapbox and make grand pronouncements in poetry. It's not that I shy away from major themes—reportedly, life, death, love, suffering—but I do shy away from making pronouncements about them. I feel that if I'm going to make a pronouncement, why don't I write an essay or a speech? My main interest in writing is not to make pronouncements anyway. But the taking on of a very large complicated structure in a long poem is made even more difficult than it would be ordinarily. To write something good and beautiful, and to do it in a new way—that's hard enough. But when I have the underlying feeling that it's wrong for me to "go grand," perhaps it's the gravity of social class tugging me down from the big structure that I might want to erect.

Berrigan, a graduate not of Columbia, but of Tulsa University, had an even stronger sense of class limits. He admired the elegance of John Ashbery, Frank O'Hara, Kenneth Koch, Edwin Denby, and James Schuyler—and realized that it was not his strength. Instead, he thought of himself as "loutish," a swaggering Irish guy who compensated for a lack of refinement by a totally incredible energy. One day I ran into Ted and his pal, the poet Steve Carey, who were waiting for a bus. It was one of those New York City February days when it snows and rains in the same cutting wind. All three of us were wearing light jackets and hatless. I had recently married and was wearing a new pair of leather gloves. After we said hello, Ted joshed, "New gloves? Louise give them to you? Soon you'll be wearing a hat! And then . . . you'll have an umbrella!"

His class loyalties were pronounced and unabashed, but he acknowledged the complexities of human aspiration. In a lecture given at the Naropa Institute, he remarked,

In the long ago past, poetry was a court activity. . . . The ladies-in-waiting and the hand-maidens and the courtiers and the friends of the duke and the king and so on, they all wrote poetry. In China and in Japan and in the European countries, it was expected of you that you do that. It was somewhat of a surprise when someone like Shakespeare, say, wrote poetry. But it wasn't too much of a surprise, because being an attractive youth and being attracted to members of the court, he aspired to that kind of social circle . . . and then there were the peasants who had hoed the field all day. Now they didn't write any poetry. You don't write any poetry if you hoe the field all day. 'Cause at night you're tired. And besides the people in the court come and take away two-thirds of what you hoe, so that they can write poetry some of the time.

That's one of the reasons that poetry is a business; it's a full-time business; it doesn't take up all your time the way working in the A&P may take up all your time, because you don't have to be on the job in that respect all the time; you don't have to go there and be there for so many hours a day and come out. But being a poet is a twenty-four-hour-a-day-thing. (*On the Level Everyday*, 51–52)

The ambitions that Ted ascribes to Shakespeare in this lecture may have reflected his own relations to the courtly social circle of his heroes O'Hara, Ashbery, and Koch—whom James Schuyler called the Harvard Wits. Speaking about Frank O'Hara, Berrigan said,

He was open to everything, of course. He was the most open person I ever met. Much more open even than Paul Blackburn, who thought of himself as very open but had a natural aversion to people who seemed like they were from some elegant minority: the way that Frank O'Hara and Kenneth Koch and John Ashbery must have seemed to him. . . . [B]ut they didn't seem that way to me. I wasn't bothered by it in the least. (*Talking in Tranquility*, 48–49)

Again, O'Hara and Blackburn are made class representatives, but this time the working-class guy chooses the open model of O'Hara over class resentments, though Ted also liked to boast about the time he knocked Kenneth Koch down at a party where they competed for a young woman's attentions—the classic working-class response to the silver-tongued ladies' man. Maybe it was because the stamp of class was so evident in Ted's speech, mannerisms, and dress that he felt little urge to proclaim his affiliations, that instead he devoted so much of his life to proclaiming the merits of that "elegant minority," the New York school. The poems of Alice Notley, who was married to Berrigan and shared the trials of their bohemian poverty, are much more outspoken about class resentments. But Berrigan did address the following lines to his brother-in-law in 1979:

> from the
> next year on, Jr-High School, on into & thru
> High School, at various jobs, thru one
> semester at Catholic Providence College, then
> 3 years in the Army, Korea, and return
> to College in Tulsa, Oklahoma (1957) right
> up to about 1960, no matter where I
> was, in what situation, with the exception of
> on the football playground, in card games, and at
> home, reading, I didn't
> know the language and I didn't know
> the rules; and naturally I didn't
> know what it was I didn't know, nor
> therefore, what was it I did know, be-
> cause I did know *something*. In the
> army I began to learn about knowing
> the rules, and so about myself and rules.
> Back in College, while easing
> into knowing the rules & what to do with that,
> I evidently had begun *hearing* the language. In

1960, & from then on, I got hit by that special
useful sense that one could, easily, anytime or where,
pick up, & so "know" the language *and* the rules. It
all had to do with Surface, and it didn't have
to be shallow.

(Talking in Tranquility, 170)

Alienation arrives with the self-consciousness of adolescence, the growing awareness of class difference and individual befuddlement about social expectations. It is only when he begins "*hearing* the language" that the young Berrigan begins to "know" the "language *and* the rules"—and to write poetry. Though the subtext is class, the dynamic is particular.

Around 1976 a poet friend (who must have been tiring of my enthusiasm for Ted Berrigan's work) warned me not to be fooled, that Berrigan was only a "literary man in blue jeans." While I appreciated the wit of the comment, I did not find the judgment so scathing. Somehow the adjective lost any effete implications when applied to Ted Berrigan's often disheveled, sometimes threadbare clothes, and a profounder political critique was blunted by my own confusions. Surely I had no sympathy for any political program that couldn't accommodate such a figure—or underestimated the liberating possibilities of aesthetic joy.

Yet it's significant that though Berrigan and Padgett never obscured their origins, and have suffered occasional critical disdain because of them, they felt that the kind of poems they wrote distanced themselves from the people they grew up among. Berrigan's assertion that the peasants didn't write poetry, for instance, could be contested by pointing to the folk music that Berrigan himself cherished and spoke about often. Forty years earlier, in the pages of the *New Masses*, Lee Hays made precisely such a case, chiding those poets who showed traces of reading

T. S. Eliot and Hart Crane, and celebrating instead the songs heard in union halls and on picket lines. But Berrigan was discriminating precisely between forms, just as Padgett did when he told me, "The very fact that Ted and I became poets and especially the kind of poets we became, that is, not traditional poets—we didn't write 'The Cremation of Sam McGee'—ejected us from our class." They believed that they could remain artists within their class only by accepting folk or popular conventions. To move beyond those conventions destined them to a place neither outside nor inside the class into which they were born. To complete the Padgett quote,

> So it's very interesting to have grown up in a certain class and still feel in many ways that it made you who you are, and yet know that you can never really be a part of it again because of your interest in art and writing. It's really weird. And one's writing continues to be influenced by—not only by the origins, but by the knowledge of the distance between you and your origins. So it's not only the presence of the class, it's the absence of the class at the same time.

What some might see as class denial, or at least irresponsibility, has always struck me as visionary optimism. Because they remain open to inspiration from any source, Berrigan's and Padgett's poems are stunning hybrids of sensibilities, traditions, possibilities, imaginations. Hart Crane, frequently insecure about his own lack of a college education, awkwardly called this quality "alert blindness"; the Cockney Keats more mellifluously termed it negative capability. It's a refusal to filter particulars according to preconceptions, to order by classification, to class off. Its products are motley and democratic, though seldom smooth and never homogenized. Shaggy commingles with combed. Every imaginative speaker alters and refines each dialect. The language constantly changes. At the same time, its history informs everything the poet writes.

Burning Beauty
Diane Wakoski, Eileen Myles,
Wilma Elizabeth McDaniel,
Tracie Morris

*W*hen Lucille Clifton was at Dartmouth College to read in October 1999, I was invited to lunch with her, Grace Paley, and three other poets from the Dartmouth faculty—William Cook, Cleopatra Mathis, and Cynthia Huntington. When Cynthia mentioned that I was writing a book about poetry and social class, Lucille turned to me and said, "I'd be interested to read that book. You know, I'm not supposed to be here myself." As a sign of the times, or maybe Dartmouth's particular dynamics, it was a remark with resonance for everyone in that company.

The major obstacle to discussing class and poetry is the lack of vocabulary. As Senator John Edwards campaigned for the Democratic Party's nomination for the presidency in September 2003, his wife Elizabeth mentioned proudly that "as the son of a South Carolina mill worker, her husband grew up without class consciousness." She went on to say that he understood the "workingman's" problems because "at his core, he is one." Then she again cited his "lack of class consciousness as his greatest tool to overcome such problems." The contradictions in Ms.

Edwards's remarks illustrate a peculiar American sensitivity to the vocabulary of class. Anyone who thinks of himself as a workingman "at his core" obviously possesses class consciousness, but does he have words to describe it?

On my first day of teaching at a community college in Vermont, I wrote my phone number on the board so students could contact me outside school hours. Because I had only recently moved to the area from New York City, I was surprised to hear a low rumble of laughter, and then outright, "Isn't that a Norwich number?" We had moved to a town with a reputation for good schools—and the high property taxes to pay for them—a town most of the community college students could not afford to live in. There were students in those classes who received some form of public assistance; many attended class at the end of an eight- or twelve-hour work day. Yet in five years of teaching at that community college, never did I hear students describe themselves as anything other than middle class.

As would my parents. My mother and stepfather sold their home and moving business when his legs grew too old to lug refrigerators up and down stairs, and moved to Florida, where they worked for many years managing a condominium, before semiretiring to a one-room condo upstairs. Semiretirement, because she continued to work as a substitute manager at several places on the beach, and he occasionally mowed lawns or cleaned pools. When they retired, they thought they could survive on savings and social security, but realized quickly that they couldn't afford medical insurance. Now they are enrolled in a managed care plan, and complain endlessly about the quality of the treatment they receive. When she prepares me to meet her acquaintances, my mother, who is outgoing and inclusive by nature, approaches the subject of class directly. "You will like them," she tells me. "They're our kind of people. Nothing pretentious or stuck up." When my mother-in-law visited, my mother noted that "Barbara is so nice you'd never guess she has a Ph.D."

Some years ago I reviewed *Emerald Ice*, selected poems by Diane Wakoski, a book that demanded to be treated in terms of its class attitudes. There was no other way to understand Wakoski's burning grudges—against Anne Sexton, against attractive women with large, light-filled kitchens, against thin homosexuals with a sense of style, and finally—though with self-conscious complexity—against beauty.

> I want to tell you
> that beauty itself
> creates injustice,
> and that while everyone suffers,
> only beauty is allowed any mercy
> from the suffering.
> I have said it before,
> the ones who need love most
> are the unlovable.
> And how much more difficult to be ugly and sensitive and still
>   to survive?   ("How Do You Tell a Story?" 302)

I'm an experienced reader of poetry who has learned to appreciate the classics of our culture despite the xenophobia, misogyny, racism, and class bias that infect them. In this case, however, I found myself for the first time looking in a mirror, where the reflection reminded me not just of Savonarola, the monk who purged Florence of its vanities by large bonfires, but of myself at sixteen.

For those of us from the working class, beauty must always remain suspect. We associate it easily with well-dressed, expensively perfumed women and men sipping champagne while they chat about the threat of the great unwashed. When I was in high school, the local symphony orchestra made free tickets available to secondary-school students. I remember accepting one, then having to attend alone when at the last minute my friends predictably found other things to do. But I wanted to go, to hear for the first time live the music I had only heard on movie sound-tracks or rare moments on television (if there was a radio station in our town devoted to classical music, I didn't know about it). Once the music began, I very much enjoyed myself, but mostly I remember feeling underdressed as I stood gawking at the beautiful bare-shouldered ladies.

About Anne Sexton, Wakoski continues:

> And I think of the lady in question,
> who did not, in fact, have to give poetry readings,
> who was, in fact, moderately wealthy, who had,
> in fact, already won many honors in that stingy world of poetry
> and who could only have had one reason for doing something
>   so painful to her
> that it made her kill herself,
> and that reason is one that I,
> wearing my daily mask of horror, will never understand /
>   perhaps,
> if you are born beautiful,
> you are allowed to be
> a fool?
> And even win prizes for it?
> While those of us
> in our round-mouthed, deep-eyed masks
> must survive,
> because actually, no one would care
> if we did not.
>   ("How Do You Tell a Story?" 301)

In another poem, titled "Joyce Carol Oates Plays the Saturn Piano," the grudge isn't personal but projected:

> How I hated the rich girls in my classes
> who were being
> expensively
> psychoanalysed (how I needed to tell

my histories),
and who played Bach
sitting decorously, neatly, on the piano bench
like little hair brushes,
while I grimaced and swayed and rocked on the bench
with each cadence, until my practice room
must have seemed like
an exercise cell for some crippled gymnast,
one who had to do all her exercises sitting
in a single position.

      ("Joyce Carol Oates Plays the Saturn Piano," 340)

At the time I wrote the review, I was embarrassed by these class resentments. They did not indicate the poet's self-proclaimed "sensitivity," but were coarse and all too familiar expressions of attitudes common to the class into which she and I were born. Furthermore, they made *us* sound pathetic and deprived. Not only did my own lucky upbringing convince me that though we didn't have money for dinner in a restaurant or nice winter coats, there were compensations and many pleasures, but my class loyalties forbade complaining to strangers. I wrote:

> Class is still among the most undiscussed subjects when writing about poetry. What Wakoski says is often distasteful and, as I believe she would be first to admit, ugly. But she pronounces an unyielding, sad truth, that the ordinary claims of ego and envy can be more powerful than the beauty created by Chopin or Beethoven. All happy instances of beauty are vulnerable to the attacks of a jealous, inflexible justice. Because we recognize pain and deprivation as sources for such notions, they sometimes have the power to elicit our sympathy and complicity. It's a bitter fruit this cactus bears, but for those of us from the lower classes, I'm afraid it's not at all exotic.
>
>   (*American Book Review*, Sept. 1990)

Reading Wakoski's poems ten years later, I'm less conscious of the grating resentment than the frustrated yearning for transformation that carries throughout a body of poems written over more than thirty years. Though ostensibly the poems proclaim the injustice of beauty, they do not, finally, argue any preference for justice, only a desire to be among those unjustly blessed.

After I moved to New York City in 1974, one of my first poet friends was Eileen Myles. We attended many of the same readings, discovered in endless barroom and coffee shop conversations that we admired many of the same poets, and established early in our friendship that we shared similar class backgrounds and had both attended commuter colleges. One evening we were chatting with two young editors of *L=A=N=G=U=A=G=E* magazine in Jim Brodey's kitchen on the Lower East Side, while everyone else crowded into Jim's bedroom to watch the Academy Awards ceremony. The editors were bright, exciting young guys and everyone seemed to be invigorated by the company until one asked us where we had gone to college. When Eileen responded UMass-Boston, both replied that they knew it well. While at Harvard, they had spent many hours there "trying to organize the working-class kids." They laughed as they recalled their naive belief that the "working class" students would be more receptive to their organizing efforts than their Ivy League classmates. Instead, they had been confounded by what they deemed the apathy of the students, and asked Eileen if she could explain. She did: "Of course we had little time for politics. We weren't just going to school. Most of us had to work!" The subject was quickly changed and we found more amiable topics to talk about. But Eileen couldn't forgive their faux pas. After the party, she and I continued drinking until the bars closed, then moved on to an all-night coffee shop on Bleecker Street, where again and again she returned to the subject of the Harvard boys and the condescension that inevitably doomed their well-intended organizing efforts.

I was reminded of the incident again as I read Eileen's "nonfiction novel" *Cool for You*, published in 2000. This is the way she prefaces remarks about her grandmother's many years in a state mental hospital:

> I'm grateful to the state of Massachusetts . . . for giving me a high quality low tuition public education. I would not be a writer if not for the University of Massachusetts (Boston). I think this is the place to thank the state. (143)

When Robert Lowell died, Eileen responded with this eulogy:

ON THE DEATH OF ROBERT LOWELL

O, I don't give a shit.
He was an old white haired man
Insensate beyond belief and
Filled with much anxiety about his imagined
Pain. Not that I'd know.
I hate fucking wasps.
The guy was a loon.
Signed up for the Spring Semester at MacLeans
A really lush retreat among pines and
Hippy attendants. Ray Charles also
Once rested there.
So did James Taylor . . .
The famous, as we know, are nuts.
Take Robert Lowell.
The old white haired coot.
Fucking dead.

(Fresh Young Voice, 28)

Though I laughed when I first heard the poem read, it also made me uncomfortable. Henry Louis Gates Jr. wrote that racism reveals at the least a failure of imagination. That's the way I felt about this poem by someone I regard as an imaginative poetic original—and one whom I knew at the time to be inspired by the poetry of John Ashbery and James Schuyler. But then again, Myles identifies herself as the child of "post-World War II working-class Bostonians," and I'm not from Boston. Those who would suggest that poems such as this are undertheorized might want to reconsider the precision of its geographical referents. The poem may be parochial, but within a few words expresses a lot of pain and anger rising from oppressive ethnic, gender, class, and aesthetic hierarchies.

Like Wakoski, Myles is fiercely individualistic in her career ambitions, but her career has been rooted in a series of strong communal identities, however serial or overlapping. Former director of the St. Mark's Poetry Project, known for its Lower East Side bohemian camaraderie, Myles gained a wider reputation as the outspoken lesbian author of *Sappho's Boat* (titled, according to Myles, to assure that a Village gay bookstore would carry it), became an improvisational and entrepreneurial stand-up artist on the downtown performance scene, and an emphatic presence in the Provincetown summer arts community.

When she published her first book with Black Sparrow Press, I heard several people remark that she would be promoted as a "female Charles Bukowski." Black Sparrow was long Bukowski's publisher, so the remark surely owed much to that, but the comparison was also fraught with class comparisons. Bukowski's depictions of life on the margins and his notorious contempt for bourgeois values deserve their own essay, but they are crude and sentimental when compared to Myles's tonic imagination. Her essay "The End of New England" presents reflections on class (and specifically, New England working class) that are far more sophisticated, sympathetic, and nimble than Bukowski's heavy hands could muster. And though Myles may resemble Bukowski in her pugnacious anger, delight in shock, deft satire, and self-abasing Bohemian parodies, the aesthetic demands of her poems are far more exacting. In her talk "The Lesbian Poet," she said:

> [I]t was poetry or the poetics of it that I was needing to address and I've hardly been anywhere other and I want to honor the place that I stand. . . . I came out here as a poet and a dyke maybe

all in one reading. . . . A lesbian is just an idea. An aesthetic one perhaps. Hugh Kenner explains that Sappho is the standard for each poetic age. . . . [I]t may not be true, but I buy it. (*School of Fish*, 123–25)

Myles's loyalties and sense of community differ drastically from Bukowski's individualist pathos. Though you can still hear working-class Boston in her voice, you also hear a poet sophisticated by her wide reading. The combination results in evasive and elliptical aesthetic and emotional strategies that quicken her poems and help them escape narrow definition.

Two of the toughest, but also most generous voices of the working class during the last half-century, have belonged to Lucille Clifton and Wilma Elizabeth McDaniel. Clifton and McDaniel differ from many of the poets mentioned in this book in that they have maintained a strong sense of working-class community. Clifton's class concerns are most notable in her early books of poems and in her crystalline memoir of the family to which she has retained strong ties. Being African American and coming of age during the midcentury crusade for civil rights, Clifton was blessed with a defining communal sense of her "people," a sense of belonging that has slipped away from many working-class Americans during the second half of the century.

Though Wilma McDaniel, now past eighty, has been writing poems since childhood, her first book wasn't published until 1973, when she was fifty-five years old. She received a modest flourish of attention and honors only lately. In reply to a request for an autobiographical note for Janet Zandy's anthology *Liberating Memory: Our Work and Our Working-Class Consciousness*, McDaniel replied:

It is strange that quite a bit is written about my poetry, read in schools, but so *little* is being *published* outside of small presses such as Hanging Loose in Brooklyn, or the feminist *Broomstick* in San Francisco. I feel almost certain that you will receive few entries from cotton-picking poets, two-room school academics, but let 'er rip. I'm coughing up postage. (210)

As Clifton's poems gain power and scope from her identification with a larger community, so the interest in McDaniel owes something to the community that she represents. McDaniel was a teenager when her Okie family fled the Dust Bowl during the depression and journeyed to California to do farmwork. She has continued to return to those years again and again in her poems, as if everything since has been slightly anticlimactic and disappointing. One feels she misses those days of her youth, perhaps the last time in anyone's memory that the working class was represented in American popular culture as a class—before the leveling explosion of television, before the McCarthy era intimidated union leaders and branded the articulation of class politics as unpatriotic. Isn't that why recent academic studies by Cary Nelson, Constance Coiner, Alan Wald, and others into working-class culture are so weighted toward the decade of the 1930s, when there was some sort of Popular Front and even Hollywood nodded toward class in *The Grapes of Wrath*?

Though I have admired McDaniel's poems since I first began to read them, I suspect that the recent academic interest in her work owes much to this nostalgia for a time when working-class identity led to political solidarity. McDaniel has responded to this recognition with modesty, grace, and bemusement. Her recent poems frequently nestle mentions of her academic appearances among more typical tales of her farmworker neighbors and family. She has never moved away from the community that is so dear and vital to her, and her portraits of her friends, neighbors, and family are sympathetic, but never in soft focus. Nor has her perspective changed significantly during the last half-century. Her poems still imply the virtues of radical redistributive politics within an encompassing framework of Christian devotion. It's a representation of working-class beliefs with economic implications always ignored by political conservatives, and social implications that often discomfort liberal professionals.

BIBLE STORIES
Buster's favorite Bible story:
how Peter caught a fish
with money in its mouth
when Jesus told him to pay
the Roman taxes

Buster didn't see how fish
could swallow coins that big
Mama told him nothing was
too hard for the Lord

Uncle Prez joked
He wished the Lord
would send *us* a school of fish
with silver dollars
in their mouths
Mama was very quiet
I could tell she didn't like
his remark
the way she looked at him
and closed the Bible

(*The Last Dust Storm*, 12)

Though her class loyalties have remained constant, McDaniel's passion for reading has inevitably broadened her sensibilities. She continues to find something especially amusing about academics, and her vigilant ear misses nothing.

TWO HELENS
As our school principal escorted him out to the bleachers for the big game, I overheard the visiting professor say he taught Greek at Berkeley.

The professor didn't look much like a sports enthusiast. He was scrawny, with a bread dough personality. But I have to say he had a quick eye for the girls.

About that time our number one cheerleader Helen Boles led her pom-pom girls out on the field. She was a raven-haired beauty, easily the most gorgeous girl at LHS.

The principal said "Here comes Helen, our own homecoming queen." The doughy professor straightened up and said with real conviction, "Helen of Troy never looked this good."

The principal was pleased and said modestly, "Helen of Troy might have launched a thousand ships, but she couldn't have inspired the *Gauchos* the way our Helen has." (*Borrowed Coats*, 80)

Class is but one of the many intersecting circles that locate us in the Boolean algebra of society. As E. P. Thompson wrote in his preface to *The Making of the English Working Class:*

If we stop history at a given point, then there are no classes but simply a multitude of individuals with a multitude of experiences. But if we watch these men [*sic*] over an adequate period of social change, we observe patterns in their relationships, their ideas, and their institutions. Class is defined by men as they live their own history, and, in the end, this is its only definition. (11)

McDaniel's poems testify unflinchingly to the lasting class disparities in American society, even as she refuses to reconcile herself to them as an inevitable feature of American life. But her poems also remind me that the distance between the rural and urban can be as bracing as the distance between social classes.

Though poets such as Wilma McDaniel who earn acclaim late in life inspire those of us who labor long and in relative anonymity, there's no substitute for early success. While the octogenarian McDaniel continues to write poems about life in the San Joaquin

Valley of California, Tracie Morris gained attention as a "hip-hop" performance poet competing in slams at the Nuyorican Café and other New York venues. Morris is a bright, attractive young woman from Brooklyn whose stylish wordplay owes more to Dr. Seuss than to Dr. Johnson. The slam phenomenon has its own demands. In accord with the tastes of the young, hip audience that frequents them, Morris's most popular poems are overtly sexual in subject, raw in expression, and not overcomplicated or delicate in treatment. (When I asked one former slam winner the secret of her own success, she joked, "A very low cut neckline.") Though Morris's poems also have a strong political inflection, works such as "Ten Men" are characterized primarily by a crowd-pleasing braggadocio reminiscent of Mayakovsky. In even her earliest poems, as in her well-known "Project Princess," there is also a pronounced sense of social class.

> Teeny feet rock
> Layered double socks
>
> Popping side piping,
> Many colored loose lace-ups
>
> Racing toe keeps up
> With fancy free gear
>
> Slick slide just pressed
> Recently weaved hair
>
> Jeans oversized belie her
> hips, back thighs
>
> That have made guys sigh
> for milleni-year.
>
> Topped by an attractive jacket:
> her suit's not for flacking flunkies
>
> Junkies or punk homies
> on the stroll.

Her hands mobile thrones
Of today's urban goddess

Clinking rings link up dragon fingers
No need to be modest!

One or two gap teeth coolin'
Sport gold initials

Doubt you get to her name
Check from the side, please chill

Color woman variation
Reworks the French twist

W/ crinkle-cut platinum frosted bangs
From a spray can's mist

Never dissed she insists: "No you
Can't touch this." And, if pissed

Bedecked fist stops boys
Who feel they must persist.

She's the one, give her some
Under fire, smoking gun

Of which raps are spun
Songs are sung

The bells are rung, rocked
Pistols cocked, unwanted

Advances blocked, well-stacked
She's jock. It's all about you

It's all about you, girl. It's all
About you and living in your world

You go on
Don't ya dare stop.

The visibility that comes with early success brings with it
opportunities and pressures. Some flinch from those opportuni-

ties and retreat to what they know well. They go on reciting the same poem or even writing a minor variant on it for the remainder of their careers. Morris responded to her opportunities by accepting an array of challenges, replying with texts "for placement in theatrical settings" that included dance, one-woman performance, songs, poems, even lectures. Her work expanded in range and ambition, and if there was an occasional scattering of focus, the growth (from an already strong base) was startling. I first met Morris when we participated on a panel devoted to poetry and social class. Billed as the hip-hop phenom among older, more traditional poets, she was as fresh and electric as promised, but impressed also by the thoughtful, carefully articulated nature of her comments. Living outside New York for the past ten years, I have had the opportunity to catch her performances only intermittently. But each time I have seen her, I have been impressed by dazzling leaps in the maturity and sophistication of her art.

Morris distinguishes between her "page work" and her "stage stuff," but to the reader (or audience) the distinctions are along a continuum—the paper work jazzed by the orality of performance, the performance work growing more adventurous in vocabulary and more syntactically complex. Like slightly older slam poets such as Paul Beatty and Julie Patton, Morris's "stage stuff" was always condensed sufficiently to retain interest on the page—except for rare sound effects and repetitions that perform strongly but can be tedious to read. In fact, her terse, compressed sense of line often reminds me of Lorine Niedecker. But Morris's magical ear now hears a greater array of muses. Without sacrificing class consciousness or political edge, she seems to daily expand resources for her imagination and voice.

> even when Ali needed mo' machismo
> he put dopes on the rope with a
> butterfly float, flippant wrist
> let loose noose's grip

like we girls did
reworking the kinetics
left-turn, right-turn
over-hand aesthetics

feet thinking double-time
meter reason school's
in season, flip in, flouncing
guild's lilies

dust clouds breezes—
ten little drummers
summon up old stories
speak in tongues

(From "Las Brujitas," Morris, *Intermission*, 33)

For all her early success, Morris, like many working-class poets, might be considered a late developer. She remains a committed student of poetry who reveals the range of her studies in frequent acknowledgments of her predecessors, as in her poem "Writers are my Nepenthe." It was only in her twenties, however, as an already accomplished poet, that she was introduced to some of the texts that we assume poets such as James Merrill or John Ashbery read closely as teens. As a result of their wide reading, in their earliest poems those precocious poets already seem full-fledged. Though Morris was precocious in her own way, by the measure of her later work we can see that when she wrote the early work, she was still en route. In poems such as "Writer's Delight," what might seem self-consciously literary in others only emphasizes the expansion of her ambitions. Where most working-class poets, as Ron Padgett suggests, avoid "large claims" for fear of sounding pretentious, Morris's extensive experience reciting before a wide range of audiences has allowed her to develop the gift of

Pushing the envelope
while moving through the crowd.

(52)

127

Seventy years ago Christopher Caudwell wrote,

> The poet finds his full individuation in bourgeois poetry, where chanted lyrical poetry becomes written study poetry, and the social ego of poetry is identified with the free individual. (290)

In Caudwell's determinist analysis, poetry evolved historically from chanted communal to written individual expression. A counterargument might now be made that the "chanted lyrical poetry" of poetry slams resurrects a public poetry for a postmodern culture that is increasingly oral, rather than literary. If so, does this mark a moment when individuals from any background can discover their free individuality, or the moment when the individuated consciousness gives way to unindividuated group identity?

A combination of serious poetic experimentation and populist crowd-pleasing is an ambition realized fully by only a few, though the tradition seems more insistent among African American poets, from Langston Hughes through Jayne Cortez. But every poetic revival in this country has been rooted in the promise of increased access. Anyone old enough to have witnessed the aftermath of the Beat explosion can recall dreadful saloon recitations by wannabes unconsciously parodying *Howl*. Anyone who attends contemporary slams appreciates how quickly innovation can become formalized and debased. Yet this vulgarized open platform, with its jarring lack of quality control, remains the most welcoming route to poetry for many. Refined in such fires, Tracie Morris now pushes the envelope in a dazzling range of experimental and traditional forms without ever seeming precious or unentitled.

Afterword

As I was finishing the last chapter of this manuscript, coal miners digging in Somerset, Pennsylvania, broke through to an abandoned shaft filled with perhaps fifty million gallons of groundwater. As the water inundated the hole in which they were working, most of the miners scrambled to safety, often wading or swimming as much as an underground mile through water up to their necks. Nine miners didn't make it, but were trapped inside an air chamber 240 feet below ground that was approximately 4 feet high and 70 feet long. As hours grew to days, rescuers attempted to drill a hole large enough to rescue any of the nine who might have survived the cold wet conditions, hunger, and thirst. Communication was finally established with the trapped miners on the third night of rescue efforts, when a phone was dropped into the hole and a trapped miner exclaimed, "What took you so long?"

Tom Wayman wrote a poem titled "The Country of Every-day: Literary Criticism" that ends:

When the poet goes out for a walk in the dusk
listening to his feet on the concrete, pondering
all of the adjectives for rain, he is walking on work
of another kind, and on lives that wear down like cement.
Somewhere a man is saying, "Worked twenty years for the City

but I'm retired now."
Sitting alone in a room, in the poorhouse of a pension
he has never read a modern poem.

(Oresick and Coles, 237)

I don't know anyone who confuses writing poetry and mining coal. One of my first experiences of work was in a ready-mix concrete plant, and though there were hot, humid south Ohio days when the dust caked in your hair or the handling of concrete blocks reduced your arms to wobbly rubber, I was young enough to play baseball in the evenings. Maybe if I had grown old doing that work, it would have consumed more of my energies. But jobs never filled the lives of my working-class uncles, who remained strong family men and also great sports. Several of them sang and played guitar in bars on evenings and weekends.

After acknowledging that we walk on the work of others, what are the implications? Would the miners be better off in a world without poems, even those unsympathetic to their plight? Some miners said after the rescue that they would never go below earth again; others said they loved their jobs and would continue at them. How many would exchange those jobs for the wages earned or the type of work performed by poets? (Of course, it's a joke to speak of the wages of poets unattached to some college or university.) Sharon O'Dair's provocative *Class, Critics, and Shakespeare* includes a chapter about a town in Oregon where a Shakespeare festival has replaced logging as the leading economic engine. O'Dair contends that many of the former loggers resent the transition from logging town to cultural resort, both because of the lower wages available to them *and* the inferior status that the proud loggers associate with service and cultural work (in the particular instance, aggravated by the nonunion nature of most of the festival's technical jobs). The working class has its own values, preferences, and exclusions, often modified by geography and local tradition.

One of my first by-lined publications was in the *Albany Times-Union*, a study of the impact that a large commercial development might have on a forested region of the Catskill Mountains. The newspaper identified the author of the report as "a local truckdriver." At the time I was working for my stepfather, who moved furniture for a living. By this time my stepfather had left the national van line he had worked for, purchased his own eighteen-foot straight truck, and worked locally. I had been doing that kind of work since I was fifteen, and liked the flexible hours offered by my stepfather's indulgence. I was unprepared for my mother's response to the article.

"They say you're a truck driver. You're not a truck driver!" she complained.

"How else would you describe me, Ma? That's what I do for a living." (I was embarrassed that she thought I had inflated my job description from helper to driver.)

"But you're not a truck driver," she insisted. "You're a college graduate."

Though I had a strong sense of social class, at that moment I realized that my mother's was more finely honed, and that because of my education, I would never again be considered working class at home—no matter how I happened to make a living.

In an article about class and culture in England, Hanif Kureishi argues that conservative Brits found the Beatles disturbing not because of any critical content in the band's banal lyrics, but because the Fab Four represented an amoral devotion to pleasure that deflected lower-class youth from a commitment to the virtues of sobriety, hard work, and gradual self-improvement. In the neighborhood I grew up in, poetry was not a career option—especially not for men. To write modern poems was so wild and unexpected a gesture that for a while I actually believed it might be revolutionary.

For seven years I edited a literary magazine, *Mag City*, with my friends Michael Scholnick and Gregory Masters. We were prickly about class and what we interpreted as condescension by those better dressed and better connected than we. Mostly we published poems that we heard recited at the Poetry Project or the Nuyorican Café. I think we would agree, however, that the highlight of our endeavor were the hours we spent in the company of poet and ballet critic Edwin Denby, in what began as an interview but was also a tender, profound tutorial by a gentleman whose origins were so far from ours as to seem like another planet.

Perhaps we must ask why we read or write poetry at all. Or perhaps we can never know. I sympathize with Wayman's retired worker, but lament that there isn't some poetry in his life. I suspect that if confronted with the poems of Ted Berrigan or Lucille Clifton, he would respond to them. But I know how tough it is to find those poems, and what barriers intervene.

This country's commitment to educating the "workforce" doesn't tear down any barriers, but continues to offer the greatest opportunity for children of working-class parents to vault one or two of those hurdles and gain some say in their own destiny. Traditional support for state colleges and universities, as well as substantial scholarships, affirmative action, and need-blind admission policies have allowed several generations of working-class youth to gain undergraduate and postgraduate educations.

In *The New Class Society*, Robert Perrucci and Earl Wysong argue persuasively that class divisions in the United States have widened since the Reagan presidency, that the prosperity enjoyed by the working class during the years following World War II has since been undermined by global commercial and industrial policies, that public services within the country have suffered, and that the education system does more to reinforce class differences and ensure the intergenerational transfer of privilege than it does to promote knowledge and extend opportunity.

Paul Kingston takes a contrary position in *The Classless Society*, insisting that the terminology of class analysis is outmoded, that because of geographic and intragenerational mobility, American society can more accurately be described in terms of stratification. Though he concedes that economic inequalities under what he calls triumphal capitalism continue to accelerate, he denies that these inequalities determine political attitudes or cultural tastes. He suggests instead that "niche" politics and marketing interfere with the development of any broad-based political movement aware of its genuine economic interests.

Lacking sociological expertise, I find aspects of both analyses convincing, but am unable to weigh the validity of either. It's alarming, however, that these contrary analyses agree on the growing inequality within American society. They agree too that the current lack of class consciousness in the country renders any immediately effective political response to this crisis unlikely. It's unsurprising that neither has much to say about poetry. Kingston writes that "about a tenth of American adults claimed to have read anything with some pretensions to literary distinction," and these "reading sophisticates are disproportionately concentrated within the ranks of the (female) upper and upper middle class" (138). Please note that even those who would substitute stratification for class must occasionally fall back upon the terminology of class to communicate with the rest of us. Note too that perhaps it's inevitable that any American who writes poetry will be considered unrepresentative of their class.

Maybe I was ruined by public education and the myths propagated by its devoted teachers. Maybe I'm nostalgic about my own library card to the Harmanus Bleecker branch of the Albany Public Library; it certainly opened worlds for me and allowed

me to read books more expensive and expansive than comics—
though I read a lot of them too. But as I glimpse what's happening in Iraq and Afghanistan, Youngstown and Flint, or Liberia,
the grand vessel of hope for Melvin Tolson, the library card
issued to young apprentice Walt Whitman still represents
opportunity. I know that reading isn't for every child, and am
not advocating a hierarchy of working-class clerks. Free loans of
musical instruments, free art materials, and free access to sports
equipment are important too. In many parts of this country, they
used to be widely available, particularly for public school students. I'm aware also that literacy can alienate you from loved
ones and even yourself. Perhaps that's what happened to
Stephen Duck or David Schubert—*after* they lost faith in their
own imaginations and succumbed to the authority of their
oppressors.

Poems may also connect. Grace Paley put it simply when she
said that "we need our imaginations to understand what is happening to other people around us, to try to understand the lives
of others" (202). Cliff Fyman's "One Busy Busboy" neither
preaches nor exhorts, but reveals the forbearing, gracious good
nature of someone doing a demanding job.

—Cliff, are you working?
—Cliff, you have a party.
—Give me one plate.
—Cliff, do you want to work this Sunday?
—How's Table 44?
—Cliff, my boy, you're going to learn something very soon.
  Trust me.
—Bring the spinach.
—Clear off Table 42. Move!
—Cliff, bring one coffee please to the guy on 31 with his back
  to here.
—Did you give that fucking guy his coffee yet?
—Would you grab this stuff off the floor?

134

—I need a wine cooler on 51.

—Cliff, put 2 Sanka 2 coffee, eh?

—When this clears up a little, kind of make this tablecloth
longer.

—Cliff, clear off Table 30.

—Cliff, you're all right.

—Cliff, pour more coffee.

—Cliff, one more coffee here!

—Bread and butter for the Chicken Lady!

—Start using your brain, ok?

—Give them 2 espressos.

—Set 53 for me real quick please?

—I said quick—that means today.

—Cliff: plates.

—Shmucko, I need a wine cooler on B, please.

—Cliff, what are you doing? Get me tartar sauce. I said tartar
sauce. Hurry.

—Cliff, there's some Mondavi white wine in there. Bring it out
to Tony for me, please?

—Eh, you give bread and butter Table 51? Use your brain.

—Eh, more butter plates.

—The coffee's cold whatever you're doing.

—Brains, brains.

—You put any amaretto in there?

—Cliff, is that fresh coffee?

—One tea, eh?

—Cliff! One tea, eh?

—Cliff, use your brain. You see cups? Put cups, put fire.

—Cliff, give me 2 Sanka 2 coffee.

—Cliff, take all this stuff inside. Never stop, never stop.

—Get a tray for your glassware.

—I think the boss went around Manhattan in a truck, rounding
up busboys off the street.

—Ashtrays, saucers come on.

—Bread and butter for 40. Right away!

—Look alive.

—Cliff, is that a clean cloth on Table 42?

—Cliff, there's a napkin on the floor under Table 51.

—Give me 4 Sanka and a tea for the lady in black. 4 Sanka and a tea for the lady in black.

—Don't forget to pick up that napkin.

—Cliff, we don't need all these ashtrays over here. With 25 ashtrays it's a little hard to work here.

—2 coffees on 30 you hear me?

—Cliff, the napkin.

—Cliff, set up 41!

—Watch it!

—Cliff, it's not 12 o'clock yet.

—Glass of water.

—Coffee on 40.

—More salad plates!

—You gave the cups on 40 but you didn't give the coffee.

—Sorry to wake you but Table 31 has to be cleared.

—Cliff, put a fresh cloth on Table 50 and one set-up for me thank you.

—Cliff, make that Table 54.

—Hi, Clipper, the boys are after you to juggle. What else do you do—card tricks?

—Cliff, take those 4 candlesticks and give them to Chuck.

—Cliff, pick up the flowers, baby.

—Cliff, right on time.

(Fyman, "One Busy Busboy," *Transfer* 5 [1990]: 106–8)

Bibliography

Preface

Coiner, Constance. *Better Red: The Writing and Resistance of Tillie Olsen and Meridel Le Sueur.* New York: Oxford University Press, 1995.

McMurtry, Larry. *Walter Benjamin at the Dairy Queen: Reflections at Sixty and Beyond.* New York: Simon and Schuster, 1999.

Nelson, Cary. *Revolutionary Memory: Recovering the Poetry of the American Left.* New York: Routledge, 2001.

Olsen, Tillie. *Silences.* New York: Delta, 1978.

Wald, Alan. *Exiles from a Future Time.* Chapel Hill: University of North Carolina Press, 2002.

Zandy, Janet, ed. *Calling Home: Working-Class Women's Writing.* New Brunswick, N.J.: Rutgers University Press, 1990.

———, ed. *Liberating Memory: Our Work and Our Working-Class Consciousness.* New Brunswick, N.J.: Rutgers University Press, 1995.

———, ed. *What We Hold in Common: An Introduction to Working-Class Studies.* New York: Feminist Press, 2001.

Introduction

Duncan, Robert. *Fictive Certainties.* New York: New Directions, 1985.

London, Jack. *Martin Eden.* New York: Macmillan 1909.

Nelson, Cary. *Repression and Recovery: Modern American Poetry and the Politics of Cultural Memory, 1910–45.* Madison: University of Wisconsin Press, 1989.

Olsen, Tillie. *Silences.* New York: Delta, 1978.

Rasula, Jed. *The American Poetry Wax Museum: Reality Effects, 1940–1990.* Urbana, Ill.: National Council of Teachers of English, 1996.

Woolf, Virginia. *A Room of One's Own.* New York: Harcourt Brace, 1929.

―――. "Women and Fiction." In *Granite and Rainbow*. London: Hogarth Press, 1958.

The "Uneducated Poets"

Barrell, John, and John Bull, eds. *The Penguin Book of Pastoral Verse*. New York: Penguin, 1982.

Drabble, Margaret, ed. *The Oxford Companion to English Literature*. 6th ed. New York: Oxford University Press, 2000.

Edwards, B. B. *Biography of Self Taught Men*. Boston: Perkins and Marvin, 1832.

Landry, Donna. *The Muses of Resistance: Laboring-Class Women's Poetry in Britain, 1739–1796*. Cambridge: Cambridge University Press, 1990.

Paffard, Michael. "Stephen Duck, the Thresher Poet." *History Today*, July 1977, 467–72.

Southey, Robert. *The Lives and Works of the Uneducated Poets*. Ed. J. S. Childers. London: H. Milford, 1925.

Waldron, Mary. *Lactilla, Milkwoman of Clifton: The Life and Writings of Ann Yearsley, 1753–1806*. Athens: University of Georgia Press, 1996.

Williams, Raymond. *The Country and the City*. New York: Oxford University Press, 1973.

A Song for Occupations

Allen, Gay Wilson. *The Solitary Singer: A Critical Biography of Walt Whitman*. Chicago: University of Chicago Press, 1985.

Burroughs, John. *Whitman: A Study*. Boston: Houghton Mifflin, 1896.

Creeley, Robert. "Preface to the Penguin Whitman." *Was That a Real Poem and Other Essays*. Bolinas, Calif.: Four Seasons, 1979.

Emerson, Ralph Waldo. *Selections from Ralph Waldo Emerson*. Ed. Steven E. Whicher. Boston: Houghton Mifflin, 1957.

Kaplan, Justin. *Walt Whitman: A Life*. New York: Simon and Schuster, 1980.

Lawrence, D. H. *Studies in Classic American Literature*. New York: Penguin, 1977.

Loving, Jerome. *Walt Whitman: The Song of Himself*. Berkeley and Los Angeles: University of California Press, 1999.

Padgett, Ron, ed. *The T&W Guide to Walt Whitman*. New York: Teachers & Writers Collaborative, 1991.

Reynolds, David. *Beneath the American Renaissance: The Subversive Imagination in the Age of Emerson and Melville*. New York: Knopf, 1988.

Reynolds, David. *Walt Whitman's America: A Cultural Biography*. New York: Vintage, 1996.

Schmidgall, Gary. *Walt Whitman: A Gay Life.* New York: Dutton, 1997.

Traubel, Horace. *With Whitman in Camden.* 6 vols. Boston: Small, Maynard, 1906–82.

Whitman, Walt. *The Collected Writings of Walt Whitman: The Journalism.* Vol. 1, *1834–1846.* Ed. Herbert Bergman, Douglas A. Noverr, and Edward J. Recchia. New York: Peter Lang, 1998.

———. *Complete Poetry and Collected Prose.* Ed. Justin Kaplan. New York: Library of America, 1982.

———. *Complete Poetry and Selected Prose.* Ed. James E. Miller Jr. Boston: Houghton Mifflin, 1959.

———. *The Neglected Walt Whitman: Vital Texts.* Ed. Sam Abrams. New York: Four Walls, Eight Windows, 1993.

———. *The Portable Walt Whitman.* Ed. Mark Van Doren, revised by Malcolm Cowley. New York: Penguin, 1979.

———. *Selected Poems, 1855–1892.* Ed. Gary Schmidgall. New York: St. Martin's, 1999.

———. *The Uncollected Poetry and Prose of Walt Whitman.* Ed. Emory Holloway. New York: Peter Smith, 1932.

Widmer, Edward. *Young America: The Flowering of Democracy in New York City.* New York: Oxford University Press, 1999.

"Poor Doc, Nobody Wants His Life or His Verses"

Beck, John. *Writing the Radical Center: William Carlos Williams, John Dewey, and American Cultural Politics.* Albany: State University of New York Press, 2001.

Cruz, Victor Hernandez. Lecture delivered at Teachers & Writers Collaborative, New York City, April 9, 1999.

Eliot, T. S. *Selected Prose of T. S. Eliot.* Ed. Frank Kermode. New York: Harcourt Brace Jovanovich, 1975.

Frail, David. *The Early Politics and Poetics of William Carlos Williams.* Ann Arbor, Mich.: UMI Research Press, 1987.

Klein, Marcus. *Foreigners: The Making of American Literature, 1900–1940.* Chicago: University of Chicago Press, 1981.

Lenhart, Gary, ed. *The Teachers & Writers Guide to William Carlos Williams.* New York: Teachers & Writers Collaborative, 1998.

Mariani, Paul. *William Carlos Williams: A New World Naked.* New York: McGraw-Hill, 1981.

———. *William Carlos Williams: The Poet and His Critics.* Chicago: American Library Association, 1975.

Miller, J. Hillis, ed. *William Carlos Williams: A Collection of Critical Essays.* Englewood Cliffs, N.J.: Prentice Hall, 1966.

Nelson, Cary. *Revolutionary Memory: Recovering the Poetry of the American Left.* New York: Routledge, 2001.

New Masses 6, nos. 5–7, October–December 1930.

Notley, Alice. *Doctor Williams' Heiresses.* Berkeley, Calif.: Tuumba Press, 1980.

Pound, Ezra. *The Literary Essays of Ezra Pound.* Ed. T. S. Eliot. New York: New Directions, 1968.

Smedman, Lorna. "Skeleton in the Closet: Williams's Debt to Gertrude Stein." *William Carlos Williams Review* 21, no. 2 (1995), 21–35.

Tashjian, Dickran. *William Carlos Williams and the American Scene, 1920–1940.* New York: Whitney Museum of American Art in association with University of California Press, 1978.

Wald, Alan. *Exiles from a Future Time.* Chapel Hill: University of North Carolina Press, 2002.

Weaver, Mike. *William Carlos Williams: The American Background.* London: Cambridge University Press, 1971.

Williams, William Carlos. "America, Whitman, and the Art of Poetry." *William Carlos Williams Review* 13, no. 1 (1987), 1–4.

———. *The Autobiography of William Carlos Williams.* New York: New Directions, 1967.

———. *I Wanted to Write a Poem: The Autobiography of the Works of a Poet.* Reported and edited by Edith Heal. New York: New Directions, 1978.

———. "Letter to an Australian Editor." *William Carlos Williams Review* 17, no. 2 (1991).

———. *Something to Say: William Carlos Williams on Younger Poets.* Ed. James E. Breslin. New York: New Directions, 1985.

"William Carlos Williams and Music, Especially Jazz." Essays by Aldon L. Nielsen, Carol Donley, Steven C. Tracy, Philip Furia, Joseph A. Coroniti. *William Carlos Williams Review* 15, no. 2 (1989).

Zukofsky, Louis. *Prepositions: The Collected Critical Essays.* Berkeley and Los Angeles: University of California, 1981.

Special Handling

Ashbery, John. *Other Traditions.* Cambridge: Harvard University Press, 2000.

"David Schubert: Works and Days." Special issue of *Quarterly Review of Literature,* 1983.

Five Young American Poets: Second Series, 1941. Norfolk, Conn.: New Directions, 1941.

Hadas, Rachel. "Eloquence, Inhabited and Uninhabited." *Parnassus* (fall–winter 1984): 133–53.

Nardi, Marcia. "Four Poems." In *New Directions* 11, ed. James Laughlin, 309–12. New York: New Directions, 1949.

———. "A Group of Poems." In *New Directions* 7, ed. James Laughlin, 413–28. New York: New Directions, 1942.

———. *Poems.* Denver: Alan Swallow Press, 1956.

O'Neil, Elizabeth Murrie, ed. *The Last Word: Letters between Marcia Nardi and William Carlos Williams.* Iowa City: University of Iowa Press, 1994.

Schubert, David. *Initial A.* New York: Macmillan, 1961.

Caviar and Cabbage

Bérubé, Michael. *Marginal Forces/Cultural Centers: Tolson, Pynchon, and the Politics of the Canon.* Ithaca: Cornell University Press, 1992.

Dove, Rita. "Telling It Like It I-S 'IS': Narrative Technique in Melvin Tolson's *Harlem Gallery.*" *New England Review and Bread Loaf Quarterly* 8, no. (1985): 109–17.

Farnsworth, Robert M. *Melvin B. Tolson, 1898–1966: Plain Talk and Poetic Prophecy.* Columbia: University of Missouri Press, 1984.

Flasch, Joy. *Melvin Tolson.* New York: Twayne, 1972.

Gates, Henry Louis, Jr., and Nellie Y. McKay, eds. *The Norton Anthology of African American Literature.* New York: Norton, 1997.

Nielsen, Aldon L. *Writing Between the Lines: Race and Intertextuality.* Athens: University of Georgia Press, 1994.

Rampersad, Arnold. *The Life of Langston Hughes.* 2 vols. New York: Oxford University Press, 1988.

Thomas, Lorenzo. *Extraordinary Measures: Afrocentric Modernism and Twentieth-Century American Poetry.* Tuscaloosa: University of Alabama Press, 2000.

Tolson, Melvin B. *Caviar and Cabbage: Selected Columns from the Washington Tribune, 1937–1944.* Ed. Robert M. Farnsworth. Columbia: University of Missouri Press, 1982.

———. *A Gallery of Harlem Portraits.* Ed. Robert M. Farnsworth. Columbia: University of Missouri Press, 1979.

———. *Harlem Gallery.* Book 1, *The Curator.* New York: Twayne, 1965.

———. *"Harlem Gallery" and Other Poems of Melvin B. Tolson.* Ed. Raymond Nelson. Charlottesville: University Press of Virginia, 1999.

———. "The Harlem Group of Negro Writers." In *Critical Essays on Langston Hughes,* ed. Edward J. Mullen. Boston: G. K. Hall, 1986.

———. *Libretto for the Republic of Liberia.* New York: Twayne, 1953.

———. "The Negro Scholar." *The Midwest Journal,* 1, no. 1 (winter 1948): 80–82.

————. "The Poetry of Melvin B. Tolson (1898–1966)." *World Literature Today* 64, no. 3 (1990): 395–400.

————. *Rendezvous with America*. New York: Dodd, Mead, 1944.

Walker, Margaret. *How I Wrote Jubilee and Other Essays on Life and Literature*. Ed. Maryemma Graham. New York: Feminist Press, 1990.

Williams, William Carlos. *Paterson*. New York: New Directions, 1963.

Opening the Field

Allen, Donald, ed. *The New American Poetry*. New York: Grove Press, 1960.

Allen, Donald, and Warren Tallman, eds. *The Poetics of the New American Poetry*. New York: Grove Press, 1973.

Bach, Gerhard, and Blaine H. Hall, eds. *Conversations with Grace Paley*. Jackson: University Press of Mississippi, 1997.

Bogan, Louise. "Verse." *New Yorker*, October 8, 1960, 197–200.

Creeley, Robert. *Collected Essays*. Berkeley and Los Angeles: University of California Press, 1989.

Ginsberg, Allen. *Deliberate Prose: Selected Essays, 1952–1995*. New York: HarperCollins, 2000.

————. *Spontaneous Mind: Selected Interviews, 1958–1996*. New York: HarperCollins, 2001.

Hall, Donald. *Death to the Death of Poetry: Essays, Reviews, Notes, Interviews*. Ann Arbor: University of Michigan Press, 1994.

————. *Poetry and Ambition: Essays, 1982–88*. Ann Arbor: University of Michigan Press, 1988.

MacGowan, Christopher, ed. *The Letters of Denise Levertov and William Carlos Williams*. New York: New Directions, 1998.

Meltzer, David, ed. *San Francisco Beat: Talking with the Poets*. San Francisco: City Lights Books, 2001.

Nielsen, Aldon Lynn. *Black Chants: Languages of African-American Postmodernism*. Cambridge: Cambridge University Press, 1997.

North, Charles. *No Other Way: Selected Prose*. Brooklyn, N.Y.: Hanging Loose, 1999.

Perloff, Marjorie. *Poetic License: Essays on Modernist and Postmodernist Lyric*. Evanston, Ill.: Northwestern University Press, 1990.

Plimpton, George, ed. *Beat Writers at Work: The Paris Review*. New York: Modern Library, 1999.

Silliman, Ron. *The New Sentence*. New York: Roof Books, 1989.

Thomas, Lorenzo. *Extraordinary Measures: Afrocentric Modernism and Twentieth-Century American Poetry*. Tuscaloosa: University of Alabama Press, 2000.

————. "The New American Poetry: After 30 Years Is It Still What's New?" *Transfer* 6 (1991): 151–56.

Thomson, Virgil. *A Virgil Thomson Reader*. Boston: Houghton Mifflin, 1981.

Tonkinson, Carole, ed. *Big Sky Mind: Buddhism and the Beat Generation*. New York: Riverhead Books, 1995.

Literary Men in Blue Jeans

Allen, Donald, ed. *The New American Poetry*. New York: Grove Press, 1960.

Allen, Donald, and George Butterick, eds. *The Postmoderns: The New American Poetry Revised*. New York: Grove Press, 1982.

Berrigan, Ted. *A Certain Slant of Sunlight*. Oakland, Calif.: O Books, 1988.

————. *In the Early Morning Rain*. London: Cape Goliard, 1970.

————. *Many Happy Returns*. New York: Corinth Press, 1969.

————. *On the Level Everyday: Selected Talks on Poetry and the Art of Living*. Ed. Joel Lewis. Jersey City, N.J.: Talisman House, 1997.

————. *Selected Poems*. New York: Penguin, 1994.

————. *So Going Around Cities: New and Selected Poems, 1958–1979*. Berkeley: Blue Wind Press, 1980.

————. *The Sonnets*. New York: Grove Press, 1964.

————. *The Sonnets*. New York: United Artists, 1982.

————. *Talking in Tranquility: Interviews with Ted Berrigan*. Ed. Stephen Ratcliffe and Leslie Scalapino. Bolinas, Calif.: Avenue B; Oakland, Calif.: O Books, 1991.

————. *Train Ride*. New York: Vehicle Editions, 1978.

Berrigan, Ted, and Ron Padgett. *Bean Spasms*. New York: Kulchur, 1967.

Berrigan, Ted, and Harris Schiff. *Yo-Yos with Money*. Henniker, N.H.: United Artists, 1979.

Clark, Tom. *Late Returns: A Memoir of Ted Berrigan*. Bolinas: Tombouctou, 1985.

Fisher, Aaron, ed. *Ted Berrigan: An Annotated Checklist*. New York: Granary Books, 1998.

Foster, Edward, ed. *Poetry and Politics in a New Millennium*. Jersey City, N.J.: Talisman House, 2000.

Hoover, Paul, ed. *Postmodern American Poetry: A Norton Anthology*. New York: Norton, 1994.

Padgett, Ron. *Blood Work: Selected Prose*. Flint, Mich.: Bamberger Books, 1993.

———. *Great Balls of Fire.* New York: Holt, Rinehart and Winston, 1969.

———. *New and Selected Poems.* Boston: David Godine, 1995.

———. *The Straight Line: Writings on Poetry and Poets.* Ann Arbor: University of Michigan Press, 2000.

———. *Ted: A Personal Memoir of Ted Berrigan.* Great Barrington, Mass.: The Figures, 1993.

———. *Toujours l'Amour.* New York: Sun, 1976.

———. *Triangles in the Afternoon.* New York: Sun, 1979.

———. *You Never Know.* Minneapolis: Coffee House, 2001.

Padgett, Ron, and Pat Padgett. Interview by Gary Lenhart. Calais, Vt., August 27, 1999.

Rifkin, Libbie. *Career Moves: Olson, Creeley, Zukofsky, Berrigan, and the American Avant-Garde.* Madison: University of Wisconsin Press, 2000.

Silliman, Ron, ed. *In the American Tree.* Orono, Maine: National Poetry Foundation, 1986.

———, ed. *In the American Tree.* Rev. ed. Orono, Maine: National Poetry Foundation, 1999.

Wald, Alan. *Exiles from a Future Time.* Chapel Hill: University of North Carolina Press, 2002.

Waldman, Anne, ed. *Nice to See You: Homage to Ted Berrigan.* Minneapolis: Coffee House, 1991.

Burning Beauty

Algarin, Miguel, and Bob Holman, eds. *Aloud! Voices from the Nuyorican Café.* New York: Henry Holt, 1994.

Caudwell, Christopher. *Illusion and Reality: A Study of the Sources of Poetry.* London: Macmillan, 1937.

Clifton, Lucille. *Blessing the Boats: New and Selected Poems, 1988–2000.* Rochester, N.Y.: BOA Editions, 2000.

———. *Good Woman: Poems and a Memoir, 1969–1980.* Brockport, N.Y.: BOA Editions, 1987.

Lemon, Ralph. *Geography: Art, Race, Exile.* With performance text by Tracie Morris. Hanover, N.H.: Wesleyan University Press, 2000.

McDaniel, Wilma Elizabeth. *Borrowed Coats.* Brooklyn, N.Y.: Hanging Loose Press, 2001.

———. *The Last Dust Storm.* Brooklyn, N.Y.: Hanging Loose Press, 1995.

———. *A Primer for Buford.* Brooklyn, N.Y.: Hanging Loose Press, 1990.

———. *Sister Vayda's Song.* Brooklyn, N.Y.: Hanging Loose Press, 1982.

Morris, Tracie. *Intermission.* New York: Soft Skull Press, 1998.

Myles, Eileen. *Cool for You.* New York: Soft Skull Press, 2000.

———. *A Fresh Young Voice from the Plains*. New York: Power Mad Press, 1981.

———. "Interview with Eileen Myles." In *Poetry and Politics in a New Millennium*, ed. Edward Foster. Jersey City, N.J.: Talisman House, 2000.

———. *Maxfield Parrish*. Santa Rosa, Calif.: Black Sparrow Press, 1995.

———. *On My Way*. Cambridge, Mass.: Faux Press, 2001.

———. *Sappho's Boat*. Los Angeles: Little Caesar Press, 1982.

———. *School of Fish*. Santa Rosa, Calif.: Black Sparrow Press, 1997.

———. *Skies*. Santa Rosa, Calif.: Black Sparrow Press, 2001.

Spillane, Megan. "Edwards: Bush at 'War on Work.'" *The Dartmouth*, 29 September 2003. www.thedartmouth.com/article.php?aid=20030 92901020.

Steedman, Carolyn Kay. *Landscape for a Good Woman: A Story of Two Lives*. New Brunswick, N.J.: Rutgers University Press, 1987.

Thompson, E. P. *The Making of the English Working Class*. London: V. Gollancz, 1963.

Wakoski, Diane. *Emerald Ice: Selected Poems, 1972–1987*. Santa Rosa, Calif.: Black Sparrow Press, 1988.

Zandy, Janet, ed. *Liberating Memory: Our Work and Our Working-Class Consciousness*. New Brunswick, N.J.: Rutgers University Press, 1995.

———, ed. *What We Hold in Common: An Introduction to Working-Class Studies*. New York: Feminist Press, 2001.

Afterword

Allison, Dorothy. *Skin: Talking about Sex, Class, and Literature*. Ithaca, N.Y.: Firebrand, 1994.

Fyman, Cliff. "One Busy Busboy." *Transfer* 5 (1990): 106–8.

Kingston, Paul. *The Classless Society*. Stanford, Calif.: Stanford University Press, 2000.

Kureishi, Hanif. *London Kills Me: Three Screenplays and Four Essays*. New York: Penguin, 1992.

O'Dair, Sharon. *Class, Critics, and Shakespeare: Bottom Lines on the Culture Wars*. Ann Arbor: University of Michigan Press, 2000.

Oresick, Peter, and Nicholas Coles. *Working Classics: Poems on Industrial Life*. Urbana: University of Illinois Press, 1990.

Paley, Grace. *Just as I Thought*. New York: Farrar, Straus and Giroux, 1998.

Perrucci, Robert, and Earl Wysong. *The New Class Society*. Lanham, Md.: Rowman and Littlefield, 1999.

Index